PETER SHAFFER was born in Liverpool, England, in 1926. During the Second World War he worked as a conscript in a coal mine; later he studied history on a scholarship to Cambridge University. From there he came to New York City, spending three years working in a bookstore and a branch of the New York Public Library. Convinced of his own uneployability, he returned to England and began writing his first play, FIVE FINGER EXERCISE, which opened in London and New York to strong critical acclaim. Then followed four other plays, which Shaffer both wrote and produced, again to widespread approval: THE PRIVATE EAR and THE PUBLIC EYE (a double bill) in 1962; THE ROYAL HUNT OF THE SUN in 1964; and BLACK COMEDY in 1965. In addition, Mr. Shaffer is the author of SHRIVINGS, which first appeared on the London stage in 1970 as THE BATTLE OF SHRIVINGS. EQUUS, his most conspicuous success to date, is the winner of the 1975 Tony Award for Best Play. Mr. Shaffer lives and works in London.

EQUUS

PETER SHAFFER

BARD BOOKS/PUBLISHED BY AVON

AVON BOOKS
A division of
The Hearst Corporation
959 Eighth Avenue
New York, New York 10019

ISBN: 0-380-00357-0

First Bard Printing, June, 1975.
Third Printing

BARD TRADEMARK REG. U.S. PAT. OFF. AND
FOREIGN COUNTRIES, REGISTERED TRADEMARK—
MARCA REGISTRADA, HECHO EN CHICAGO, U.S.A.

Printed in the U.S.A.

For PAUL
with love

EQUUS

A NOTE ON THE BOOK

What appears in this book is a description of the first production of *Equus* at the National Theatre in July 1973. In making this description, I am partly satisfying myself, but also partly bowing to demand.

When people buy the published text of a new play, they mostly want to recall the experience they received in the theatre. That experience is composed, of course, not merely of the words they heard, but the gestures they saw, and the lighting, and the look of the thing.

There are, however, evils attendant on this sort of description. It can imprison a play in one particular stylisation. Just as seriously, it can do a real injustice to the original Director, by incorporating his ideas without truly acknowledging them. Worse, if the Director is as inventive as John Dexter, it can actually seem to minimise those ideas, just by flatly setting down on paper what was far from flat on the stage, and listing inexpressively, details of his work which, in accumulation, became deeply expressive.

Dexter directs powerfully through suggestion. Into the theatrical spaces he contrives, flows the communal imagination of an audience. He enables it to charge the action of a play with electric life. He is a master of gesture and of economy. Aesthetically, his founding fathers are Noh Drama and Berthold Brecht: the plain plank; the clear light; the great pleasure in a set-piece. I do not mean by this that he would ever direct a single minute of physical action which detracted from the meaning of a play, or in some grand visual sense subverted it—he sharply dislikes effect isolated from context—but he is naturally and rightly drawn to plays which demand elaborate physical actions to complete them.

The Royal Hunt of the Sun and *Black Comedy*, both of which he directed, are such pieces: and so is *Equus*. Their visual action is to me as much a part of the play as the dialogue. I suppose my head has always been full of images. The gold masks staring hopefully and then in gathering despair at the sky, at the end of *The Royal Hunt of the Sun*, had been part of my imagination ever since I first saw a Peruvian funeral mask with its elongated eyes and red-smeared cheeks. Brindsley Miller in the lit-up darkness of *Black Comedy,* slowly moving the spiky legs of a Regency chair one inch before the innocent face of his spinster neighbour, had tiptoed that very journey in my head as I sat at my desk. But such images, like the Field of Ha-ha in *Equus* with its mist and nettles, still have to be externalised. In John Dexter's courageous and precise staging, they acquire a vibrant and unforgettable life.

While I am confessing debts, let me mention John Napier who created the tough, bright masks of horsedom; Andy Phillips who lit them superbly; and above all, Claude Chagrin, who animated them. She created, with the help of six human actors, a stable of Superhorses to stalk through the mind.

Finally, out of a fine company I must set down the names of three actors who made the first performance of this play live with a very special intensity. Alec McCowen's *Dysart* touched audiences deeply with its dry agony. Peter Firth's *Alan* left them sighing with admiration. Nicholas Clay's horse, *Nugget* was, quite simply, unforgettable.

Rehearsing a play is making the word flesh. Publishing a play is reversing the process. I can only hope this book is not too unjust to these brilliant people.

P.S.

A NOTE ON THE PLAY

One weekend over two years ago, I was driving with a friend through bleak countryside. We passed a stable. Suddenly he was reminded by it of an alarming crime which he had heard about recently at a dinner party in London. He knew only one horrible detail, and his complete mention of it could barely have lasted a minute—but it was enough to arouse in me an intense fascination.

The act had been committed several years before by a highly disturbed young man. It had deeply shocked a local bench of magistrates. It lacked, finally, any coherent explanation.

A few months later my friend died. I could not verify what he had said, or ask him to expand it. He had given me no name, no place, and no time. I don't think he knew them. All I possessed was his report of a dreadful event, and the feeling it engendered in me. I knew very strongly that I wanted to interpret it in some entirely personal way. I had to create a mental world in which the deed could be made comprehensible.

Every person and incident in *Equus* is of my own invention, save the crime itself: and even that I modified to accord with what I feel to be acceptable theatrical proportion. I am grateful now that I have never received confirmed details of the real story, since my concern has been more and more with a different kind of exploration.

I have been lucky, in doing final work on the play, to have enjoyed the advice and expert comment of a distinguished child psychiatrist. Through him I have tried to keep things real in a more naturalistic sense. I have also come to perceive that psychiatrists are an immensely varied breed, professing immensely varied methods and techniques. Martin Dysart is simply one doctor in one hospital. I must take responsibility for him, as I do for his patient.

THE SET

A square of wood set on a circle of wood.

The square resembles a railed boxing ring. The rail, also of wood, encloses three sides. It is perforated on each side by an opening. Under the rail are a few vertical slats, as if in a fence. On the downstage side there is no rail. The whole square is set on ball bearings, so that by slight pressure from actors standing round it on the circle, it can be made to turn round smoothly by hand.

On the square are set three little plain benches, also of wood. They are placed parallel with the rail, against the slats, but can be moved out by the actors to stand at right angles to them.

Set into the floor of the square, and flush with it, is a thin metal pole, about a yard high. This can be raised out of the floor, to stand upright. It acts as a support for the actor playing Nugget, when he is ridden.

In the area outside the circle stand benches. Two downstage left and right, are curved to accord with the circle. The left one is used by Dysart as a listening and observing post when he is out of the square, and also by Alan as his hospital bed. The right one is used by Alan's parents, who sit side by side on it. (Viewpoint is from the main body of the audience.)

Further benches stand upstage, and accommodate the other actors. All the cast of *Equus* sits on stage the entire evening. They get up to perform their scenes, and return when they are done to their places around the set. They are witnesses, assistants—and especially a Chorus.

Upstage, forming a backdrop to the whole, are tiers of seats in the fashion of a dissecting theatre, formed into two railed-off blocks, pierced by a central tunnel. In these blocks sit members of the audience. During the play, Dysart addresses them directly from time to time, as he addresses the main body of the theatre. No other actor ever refers to them.

To left and right, downstage, stand two ladders on which are suspended horse masks.

The colour of all benches is olive green.

Above the stage hangs a battery of lights, set in a huge metal ring. Light cues, in this version, will be only of the most general description.

CHARACTERS

MARTIN DYSART, *a psychiatrist*
ALAN STRANG
FRANK STRANG, *his father*
DORA STRANG, *his mother*
HESTHER SALOMON, *a magistrate*
JILL MASON
HARRY DALTON, *a stable owner*
A YOUNG HORSEMAN
A NURSE

SIX ACTORS—*including the Young Horseman, who also plays Nugget—appear as Horses.*

The main action of the play takes place in Rokeby Psychiatric Hospital in Southern England.

The time is the present.

The play is divided into numbered scenes, indicating a change of time or locale or mood. The action, however, is continuous.

THE HORSES

The actors wear track-suits of chestnut velvet. On their feet are light strutted hooves, about four inches high, set on metal horse-shoes. On their hands are gloves of the same colour. On their heads are tough masks made of alternating bands of silver wire and leather: their eyes are outlined by leather blinkers. The actors' own heads are seen beneath them: no attempt should be made to conceal them.

Any literalism which could suggest the cosy familiarity of a domestic animal—or worse, a pantomime horse—should be avoided. The actors should never crouch on all fours, or even bend forward. They must always—except on the one occasion where Nugget is ridden—stand upright, as if the body of the horse extended invisibly behind them. Animal effect must be created entirely mimetically, through the use of legs, knees, neck, face, and the turn of the head which can move the mask above it through all the gestures of equine wariness and pride. Great care must also be taken that the masks are put on before the audience with very precise timing—the actors watching each other, so that the masking has an exact and ceremonial effect.

THE CHORUS

References are made in the text to the Equus Noise. I have in mind a choric effect, made by all the actors sitting round upstage, and composed of humming, thumping, and stamping—though never of neighing or whinnying. This Noise heralds or illustrates the presence of Equus the God.

Equus was first presented by The National Theatre at The Old Vic Theatre on July 26, 1973, with the following cast:

MARTIN DYSART	Alec McCowen
NURSE	Louie Ramsay
HESTHER SALOMON	Gillian Barge
ALAN STRANG	Peter Firth
FRANK STRANG	Alan MacNaughtan
DORA STRANG	Jeanne Watts
HORSEMAN	Nicholas Clay
HARRY DALTON	David Healy
JILL MASON	Doran Godwin
and	

Neil Cunningham, David Graham, David Kincaid, Maggie Riley, Rosalind Shanks, Veronica Sowerby, Harry Waters

PRODUCTION	John Dexter
DESIGN	John Napier
MUSIC	Marc Wilkinson
LIGHTING	Andy Phillips
MOVEMENT	Claude Chagrin
ASSISTANT TO THE PRODUCER	Kenneth Mackintosh
STAGE MANAGER	Diana Boddington
DEPUTY STAGE MANAGERS	Phil Robins
	Tony Walters
ASSISTANT STAGE MANAGERS	Elizabeth Markham
	Terry Oliver

ACT ONE

1

Darkness.
Silence.
Dim light up on the square. In a spotlight stands Alan Strang, a lean boy of seventeen, in sweater and jeans. In front of him, the horse Nugget. Alan's pose represents a contour of great tenderness: his head is pressed against the shoulder of the horse, his hands stretching up to fondle its head. The horse in turn nuzzles his neck.
The flame of a cigarette lighter jumps in the dark. Lights come up slowly on the circle. On the left bench, downstage, Martin Dysart, smoking. A man in his mid-forties.

DYSART: With one particular horse, called Nugget, he embraces. The animal digs its sweaty brow into his cheek, and they stand in the dark for an hour—like a necking couple. And of all nonsensical things—I keep thinking about the *horse!* Not the boy: the horse, and what it may be trying to do. I keep seeing that huge head kissing him with its chained mouth. Nudging through the metal some desire absolutely irrelevant to filling its belly or propagating its own kind. What desire could that be? Not to stay a horse any longer? Not to remain reined up for ever in those particular genetic strings? Is it possible, at certain moments we cannot imagine, a horse can add its sufferings together—the non-stop jerks and jabs that are its daily life—and turn them into grief? What use is grief to a horse?

Alan leads Nugget out of the square and they disappear to-
gether up the tunnel, the horse's hooves scraping delicately
on the wood.
Dysart rises, and addresses both the large audience in the
theatre and the smaller one on stage.

You see, I'm lost. What use, I should be asking, are
questions like these to an overworked psychiatrist in a
provincial hospital? They're worse than useless: they are,
in fact, subversive.

He enters the square. The light grows brighter.

The thing is, I'm desperate. You see, I'm wearing that
horse's head myself. That's the feeling. All reined up in
old language and old assumptions, straining to jump
clean-hoofed on to a whole new track of being I only
suspect is there. I can't see it, because my educated,
average head is being held at the wrong angle. I can't
jump because the bit forbids it, and my own basic force
—my horsepower, if you like—is too little. The only
thing I know for sure is this: a horse's head is finally
unknowable to me. Yet I handle children's heads—which
I must presume to be more complicated, at least in the
area of my chief concern. . . . In a way, it has nothing
to do with this boy. The doubts have been there for
years, piling up steadily in this dreary place. It's only
the extremity of this case that's made them active. I
know that. The *extremity* is the point! All the same,
whatever the reason, they are now, these doubts, not
just vaguely worrying—but intolerable . . . I'm sorry.
I'm not making much sense. Let me start properly: in
order. It began one Monday last month, with Hesther's
visit.

2

The light gets warmer.
He sits. Nurse enters the square.

NURSE: Mrs Salomon to see you, Doctor.
DYSART: Show her in, please.

Nurse leaves and crosses to where Hesther sits.

Some days I blame Hesther. She brought him to see me.
But of course that's nonsense. What is he but a last
straw? a last symbol? If it hadn't been him, it would
have been the next patient, or the next. At least, I suppose so.

Hesther enters the square: a woman in her mid-forties.

HESTHER: Hallo, Martin.

Dysart rises and kisses her on the cheek.

DYSART: Madam Chairman! Welcome to the torture cham-
ber!
HESTHER: It's good of you to see me right away.
DYSART: You're a welcome relief. Take a couch.
HESTHER: It's been a day?
DYSART: No—just a fifteen year old schizophrenic, and a
girl of eight thrashed into catatonia by her father. Nor-
mal, really . . . You're in a state.
HESTHER: Martin, this is the most shocking case I ever
tried.
DYSART: So you said on the phone.
HESTHER: I mean it. My bench wanted to send the boy to
prison. For life, if they could manage it. It took me two
hours solid arguing to get him sent to you instead.
DYSART: Me?
HESTHER: I mean, to hospital.
DYSART: Now look, Hesther. Before you say anything else,
I can take no more patients at the moment. I can't even
cope with the ones I have.
HESTHER: You must.
DYSART: Why?
HESTHER: Because most people are going to be disgusted
by the whole thing. Including doctors.

23

DYSART: May I remind you I share this room with two highly competent psychiatrists?

HESTHER: Bennett and Thoroughgood. They'll be as shocked as the public.

DYSART: That's an absolutely unwarrantable statement.

HESTHER: Oh, they'll be cool and exact. And underneath they'll be revolted, and immovably English. Just like my bench.

DYSART: Well, what am I? Polynesian?

HESTHER: You know exactly what I mean! . . . [pause] Please, Martin. It's vital. You're this boy's only chance.

DYSART: Why? What's he done? Dosed some little girl's Pepsi with Spanish Fly? What could possibly throw your bench into two-hour convulsions?

HESTHER: He blinded six horses with a metal spike.

A long pause.

DYSART: Blinded?

HESTHER: Yes.

DYSART: All at once, or over a period?

HESTHER: All on the same night.

DYSART: Where?

HESTHER: In a riding stable near Winchester. He worked there at weekends.

DYSART: How old?

HESTHER: Seventeen.

DYSART: What did he say in Court?

HESTHER: Nothing. He just sang.

DYSART: Sang?

HESTHER: Any time anyone asked him anything.

Pause.

Please take him, Martin. It's the last favour I'll ever ask you.

DYSART: No, it's not.

HESTHER: No, it's not—and he's probably abominable. All I know is, he needs you badly. Because there really is nobody within a hundred miles of your desk who can

handle him. And perhaps understand what this is about.
Also . . . .

DYSART: What?

HESTHER: There's something very special about him.

DYSART: In what way?

HESTHER: Vibrations.

DYSART: You and your vibrations.

HESTHER: They're quite startling. You'll see.

DYSART: When does he get here?

HESTHER: Tomorrow morning. Luckily there was a bed in
Neville Ward. I know this is an awful imposition, Martin. Frankly I didn't know what else to do.

Pause.

DYSART: Can you come in and see me on Friday?

HESTHER: Bless you!

DYSART: If you come after work I can give you a drink.
Will 6.30 be all right?

HESTHER: You're a dear. You really are.

DYSART: Famous for it.

HESTHER: Goodbye.

DYSART: By the way, what's his name?

HESTHER: Alan Strang.

She leaves and returns to her seat.

DYSART: [*to audience*] What did I expect of him? Very
little, I promise you. One more dented little face. One
more adolescent freak. The usual unusual. One great
thing about being in the adjustment business: you're
never short of customers.

*Nurse comes down the tunnel, followed by Alan. She en-
ters the square.*

NURSE: Alan Strang, Doctor.

The boy comes in.

DYSART: Hallo. My name's Martin Dysart. I'm pleased to
meet you.

He puts out his hand. Alan does not respond in any way.

That'll be all, Nurse, thank you.

3

Nurse goes out and back to her place.
Dysart sits, opening a file.

So: did you have a good journey? I hope they gave you
lunch at least. Not that there's much to choose between
a British Rail meal and one here.

Alan stands staring at him.

DYSART: Won't you sit down?

Pause. He does not. Dysart consults his file.

Is this your full name? Alan Strang?

Silence.

And you're seventeen. Is that right? Seventeen? . . .
Well?

ALAN [*singing low*] Double your pleasure,
Double your fun
With Doublemint, Doublemint
Doublemint gum.

DYSART: [*unperturbed*] Now, let's see. You work in an
electrical shop during the week. You live with your
parents, and your father's a printer. What sort of things
does he print?

ALAN: [*singing louder*] Double your pleasure
Double your fun
With Doublemint, Doublemint
Doublemint gum.

DYSART: I mean does he do leaflets and calendars? Things like that?

The boy approaches him, hostile.

ALAN: [*singing*] Try the taste of Martini
The most beautiful drink in the world.
It's the right one—
The bright one—
That's Martini!
DYSART: I wish you'd sit down, if you're going to sing.
Don't you think you'd be more comfortable?

Pause.

ALAN: [*singing*] There's only one T in Typhoo!
In packets and in teabags too.
Any way you make it, you'll find it's true:
There's only one T in Typhoo!
DYSART: [*appreciatively*] Now that's a good song. I like it better than the other two. Can I hear that one again?

Alan starts away from him, and sits on the upstage bench.

ALAN: [*singing*] Double your pleasure
Double your fun
With Doublemint, Doublemint
Doublemint gum.
DYSART: [*smiling*] You know I was wrong. I really do think that one's better. It's got such a catchy tune. Please do that one again.

Silence. The boy glares at him.

I'm going to put you in a private bedroom for a little while. There are one or two available, and they're rather more pleasant than being in a ward. Will you please come and see me tomorrow? . . . [*He rises*] By the way, which parent is it who won't allow you to watch television? Mother or father? Or is it both? [*calling out of the door*] Nurse!

27

Alan stares at him. Nurse comes in.

NURSE: Yes, Doctor?

DYSART: Take Strang here to Number Three, will you? He's moving in there for a while.

NURSE: Very good, Doctor.

DYSART: [*to Alan*] You'll like that room. It's nice.

The boy sits staring at Dysart.
Dysart returns the stare.

NURSE: Come along, young man. This way. . . . I said this way, please.

Reluctantly Alan rises and goes to Nurse, passing dangerously close to Dysart, and out through the left door. Dysart looks after him, fascinated.

4

Nurse and patient move on to the circle, and walk downstage to the bench where the doctor first sat, which is to serve also as Alan's bed.

NURSE: Well now: isn't this nice? You're lucky to be in here, you know, rather than the ward. That ward's a noisy old place.

ALAN: [*singing*] Let's go where you wanna go—Texaco!

NURSE: [*contemplating him*] I hope you're not going to make a nuisance of yourself. You'll have a much better time of it here, you know, if you behave yourself.

ALAN: Fuck off.

NURSE: [*tight*] That's the bell there. The lav's down the corridor.

She leaves him, and goes back to her place.
Alan lies down.

5

Dysart stands in the middle of the square and addresses the audience. He is agitated.

DYSART: That night, I had this very explicit dream. In it I'm a chief priest in Homeric Greece. I'm wearing a wide gold mask, all noble and bearded, like the so-called Mask of Agamemnon found at Mycenae. I'm standing by a thick round stone and holding a sharp knife. In fact, I'm officiating at some immensely important ritual sacrifice, on which depends the fate of the crops or of a military expedition. The sacrifice is a herd of children: about five hundred boys and girls. I can see them stretching away in a long queue, right across the plain of Argos. I know it's Argos because of the red soil. On either side of me stand two assistant priests, wearing masks as well: lumpy, pop-eyed masks, such as also were found at Mycenae. They are enormously strong, these other priests, and absolutely tireless. As each child steps forward, they grab it from behind and throw it over the stone. Then, with a surgical skill which amazes even me, I fit in the knife and slice elegantly down to the navel, just like a seamstress following a pattern. I part the flaps, sever the inner tubes, yank them out and throw them hot and steaming on to the floor. The other two then study the pattern they make, as if they were reading hieroglyphics. It's obvious to me that I'm tops as chief priest. It's this unique talent for carving that has got me where I am. The only thing is, unknown to them, I've started to feel distinctly nauseous. And with each victim, it's getting worse. My face is going green behind the mask. Of course, I redouble my efforts to look professional—cutting and snipping for all I'm worth: mainly because I know that if ever those two assistants so much as glimpse my distress—and the implied doubt that this repetitive and smelly work is doing any social good at all—I will be the next across the stone. And then, of course—the damn mask begins to slip. The priests both turn and look at it—it slips some more—they see the green sweat running down my face—their gold pop-eyes suddenly fill up with blood—they tear the knife out of my hand . . . and I wake up.

6

Hesther enters the square. Light grows warmer.

HESTHER: That's the most indulgent thing I ever heard.

DYSART: You think?

HESTHER: Please don't be ridiculous. You've done the most superb work with children. You must know that.

DYSART: Yes, but do the children?

HESTHER: Really!

DYSART: I'm sorry.

HESTHER: So you should be.

DYSART: I don't know why you listen. It's just professional menopause. Everyone gets it sooner or later. Except you.

HESTHER: Oh, of course. I feel totally fit to be a magistrate all the time.

DYSART: No, you don't—but then that's you feeling unworthy to fill a job. I feel the job is unworthy to fill me.

HESTHER: Do you seriously?

DYSART: More and more. I'd like to spend the next ten years wandering very slowly around the *real* Greece . . . Anyway, all this dream nonsense is your fault.

HESTHER: Mine?

DYSART: It's that lad of yours who started it off. Do you know it's his face I saw on every victim across the stone?

HESTHER: Strang?

DYSART: He has the strangest stare I ever met.

HESTHER: Yes.

DYSART: It's exactly like being accused. Violently accused. But what of? . . . Treating him is going to be unsettling.

Especially in my present state. His singing was direct enough. His speech is more so.

HESTHER: [*surprised*] He's talking to you, then?

DYSART: Oh yes. It took him two more days of commercials, and then he snapped. Just like that—I suspect it has something to do with his nightmares.

Nurse walks briskly round the circle, a blanket over her arm, a clipboard of notes in her hand.

HESTHER: He has nightmares?

DYSART: Bad ones.

NURSE: We had to give him a sedative or two, Doctor. Last night it was exactly the same.

DYSART: [*to Nurse*] What does he do? Call out?

NURSE: [*to desk*] A lot of screaming, Doctor.

DYSART: [*to Nurse*] Screaming?

NURSE: One word in particular.

DYSART: [*to Nurse*] You mean a special word?

NURSE: Over and over again. [*Consulting clipboard*] It sounds like 'Ek'.

HESTHER: Ek?

NURSE: Yes, Doctor. Ek. . . . 'Ek!' he goes. 'Ek!'

HESTHER: How weird.

NURSE: When I woke him up he clung to me like he was going to break my arm.

She stops at Alan's bed. He is sitting up. She puts the blanket over him, and returns to her place.

DYSART: And then he burst in—just like that—without knocking or anything. Fortunately, I didn't have a patient with me.

ALAN: [*Jumping up*] Dad!

HESTHER: What?

DYSART: The answer to a question I'd asked him two days before. Spat out with the same anger as he sang the commercials.

HESTHER: Dad what?

ALAN: Who hates telly.

31

He lies downstage on the circle, as if watching television.

HESTHER: You mean his dad forbids him to watch?
DYSART: Yes.
ALAN: It's a dangerous drug.
HESTHER: Oh, really!

Frank stands up and enters the scene downstage on the circle. A man in his fifties.

FRANK: [*to Alan*] It may not look like that, but that's what it is. Absolutely fatal mentally, if you receive my meaning.

Dora follows him on. She is also middle-aged.

DORA: That's a little extreme, dear, isn't it?
FRANK: You sit in front of that thing long enough, you'll become stupid for life—like most of the population. [*to Alan*] The thing is, it's a *swiz*. It seems to be offering you something, but actually it's taking something away. Your intelligence and your concentration, every minute you watch it. That's a true swiz, do you see?

Seated on the floor, Alan shrugs.

I don't want to sound like a spoilsport, old chum—but there really is no substitute for reading. What's the matter: don't you like it?
ALAN: It's all right.
FRANK: I know you think it's none of my beeswax, but it really is you know . . . Actually, it's a disgrace when you come to think of it. You the son of a printer, and never opening a book! If all the world was like you, I'd be out of a job, if you receive my meaning!
DORA: All the same, times change, Frank.
FRANK [*reasonably*] They change if you let them change, Dora. Please return that set in the morning.
ALAN: [*crying out*] No!
DORA: Frank! No!
FRANK: I'm sorry, Dora, but I'm not having that thing in

32

the house a moment longer. I told you I didn't want it to begin with.

DORA: But, dear, everyone watches television these days!

FRANK: Yes, and what do they watch? Mindless violence! Mindless jokes! Every five minutes some laughing idiot selling you something you don't want, just to bolster up the economic system. [*to Alan*] I'm sorry, old chum.

He leaves the scene and sits again in his place.

HESTHER: He's a Communist, then?

DYSART: Old-type Socialist, I'd say. Relentlessly self-improving.

HESTHER: They're *both* older than you'd expect.

DYSART: So I gather.

DORA: [*looking after Frank*] Really, dear, you are very extreme!

She leaves the scene too, and again sits beside her husband.

HESTHER: She's an ex-school teacher, isn't she?

DYSART: Yes. The boy's proud of that. We got on to it this afternoon.

ALAN: [*belligerently, standing up*] She knows more than you.

Hesther crosses and sits by Dysart. During the following, the boy walks round the circle, speaking to Dysart but not looking at him. Dysart replies in the same manner.

DYSART: [*to Alan*] Does she?

ALAN: I bet I do too. I bet I know more history than you.

DYSART: [*to Alan*] Well, I bet you don't.

ALAN: All right: who was the Hammer of the Scots?

DYSART: [*to Alan*] I don't know: who?

ALAN: King Edward the First. Who never smiled again?

DYSART: [*to Alan*] I don't know: who?

ALAN: You don't know anything, do you? It was Henry the First. I know all the Kings.

DYSART: [*to Alan*] And who's your favourite?

ALAN: John.

DYSART: [to Alan] Why?

ALAN: Because he put out the eyes of that smarty little—

Pause.

[*sensing he has said something wrong*] Well, he didn't
really. He was prevented, because the gaoler was merciful!

HESTHER: Oh dear.

ALAN: *He was prevented!*

DYSART: Something odder was to follow.

ALAN: Who said 'Religion is the opium of the people'?

HESTHER: Good Lord!

Alan giggles.

DYSART: The odd thing was, he said it with a sort of guilty
snigger. The sentence is obviously associated with some
kind of tension.

HESTHER: What did you say?

DYSART: I gave him the right answer. [*to Alan*] Karl Marx.

ALAN: No.

DYSART: [*to Alan*] Then who?

ALAN: Mind your own beeswax.

DYSART: It's probably his dad. He may say it to provoke
his wife.

HESTHER: And you mean she's religious?

DYSART: She could be. I tried to discover—none too suc-
cessfully.

ALAN: Mind your own beeswax!

Alan goes back to bed and lies down in the dark.

DYSART: However, I shall find out on Sunday.

HESTHER: What do you mean?

DYSART: [*getting up*] I want to have a look at his home, so
I invited myself over.

HESTHER: Did you?

DYSART: If there's any tension over religion, it should be
evident on a Sabbath evening! I'll let you know.

He kisses her cheek and they part, both leaving the square. Hesther sits in her place again; Dysart walks round the circle, and greets Dora who stands waiting for him downstage.

7

DYSART: [*shaking hands*] Mrs Strang.

DORA: Mr Strang's still at the Press, I'm afraid. He should be home in a minute.

DYSART: He works Sundays as well?

DORA: Oh, yes. He doesn't set much store by Sundays.

DYSART: Perhaps you and I could have a little talk before he comes in.

DORA: Certainly. Won't you come into the living room?

She leads the way into the square. She is very nervous.

Please. . . .

She motions him to sit, then holds her hands tightly together.

DYSART: Mrs Strang, have you any idea how this thing could have occurred?

DORA: I can't imagine, Doctor. It's all so unbelievable! . . . Alan's always been such a gentle boy. He loves animals! Especially horses.

DYSART: Especially?

DORA: Yes. He even has a photograph of one up in his bedroom. A beautiful white one, looking over a gate. His father gave it to him a few years ago, off a calendar he'd printed—and he's never taken it down . . . And when he was seven or eight, I used to have to read him the same book over and over, all *about* a horse.

DYSART: Really?

DORA: Yes: it was called Prince, and no one could ride him.

35

Alan calls from his bed, not looking at his mother.

ALAN: [*excited, younger voice*] Why not? . . . Why not?
. . . Say it! In his voice!
DORA: He loved the idea of animals talking.
DYSART: Did he?
ALAN: *Say it! Say it! . . . Use his voice!*
DORA: [*'proud' voice*] 'Because I am faithful!'

Alan giggles.

'My name is Prince, and I'm a Prince among horses!
Only my young Master can ride me! Anyone else—I'll
throw off!'

Alan giggles louder.

And then I remember I used to tell him a funny thing
about falling off horses. Did you know that when Chris-
tian cavalry first appeared in the New World, the pagans
thought horse and rider was one person?
DYSART: Really?
ALAN: [*sitting up, amazed*] One person?
DORA: Actually they thought it must be a god.
ALAN: *A god!*
DORA: It was only when one rider fell off, they realized the
truth.
DYSART: That's fascinating. I never heard that before. . . .
Can you remember anything else like that you may have
told him about horses?
DORA: Well, not really. They're in the Bible, of course. 'He
saith among the trumpets, Ha, ha.'
DYSART: Ha, ha?
DORA: The Book of Job. Such a noble passage. *You* know
—[*quoting*] 'Hast thou given the horse strength?'
ALAN: [*responding*] 'Hast thou clothed his neck with thun-
der?'
DORA: [*to Alan*] 'The glory of his nostrils is terrible!'
ALAN: 'He swallows the ground with fierceness and rage!'
DORA: 'He saith among the trumpets—'
ALAN: [*trumpeting*] 'Ha! Ha!'

DORA: [to Dysart] Isn't that splendid?

DYSART: It certainly is.

ALAN: [trumpeting] Ha! Ha!

DORA: And then, of course, we saw an awful lot of Westerns on the television. He couldn't have enough of those.

DYSART: But surely you don't have a set, do you? I understood Mr Strang doesn't approve.

DORA: [conspiratorially] He doesn't . . . I used to let him slip off in the afternoons to a friend next door.

DYSART: [smiling] You mean without his father's knowledge?

DORA: What the eye does not see, the heart does not grieve over, does it? Anyway, Westerns are harmless enough, surely?

Frank stands up and enters the square.
Alan lies back under the blanket.

[to Frank] Oh, hallo dear. This is Dr Dysart.

FRANK: [shaking hands] How d'you do?

DYSART: How d'you do?

DORA: I was just telling the Doctor, Alan's always adored horses.

FRANK: [tight] We assumed he did.

DORA: You know he did, dear. Look how he liked that photograph you gave him.

FRANK: [startled] What about it?

DORA: Nothing dear. Just that he pestered you to have it as soon as he saw it. Do you remember? [to Dysart] We've always been a horsey family. At least my side of it has. My grandfather used to ride every morning on the downs behind Brighton, all dressed up in bowler hat and jodhpurs! He used to look splendid. Indulging in equitation, he called it.

Frank moves away from them and sits wearily.

ALAN: [trying the word] Equitation. . . .

DORA: I remember I told him how that came from *equus*, the Latin word for horse. Alan was fascinated by that word, I know. I suppose because he'd never come across one with two U's together before.

ALAN: [*savouring it*] Equus!

DORA: I always wanted the boy to ride himself. He'd have so enjoyed it.

DYSART: But surely he did?

DORA: No.

DYSART: Never?

DORA: He didn't care for it. He was most definite about not wanting to.

DYSART: But he must have had to at the stables? I mean, it would be part of the job.

DORA: You'd have thought so, but no. He absolutely wouldn't, would he, dear?

FRANK: [*dryly*] It seems he was perfectly happy raking out manure.

DYSART: Did he ever give a reason for this?

DORA: No. I must say we both thought it most peculiar, but he wouldn't discuss it. I mean, you'd have thought he'd be longing to get out in the air after being cooped up all week in that dreadful shop. Electrical and kitchenware! Isn't *that* an environment for a sensitive boy, Doctor? . . .

FRANK: Dear, have you offered the doctor a cup of tea?

DORA: Oh dear, no, I haven't! . . . And you must be dying for one.

DYSART: That would be nice.

DORA: Of course it would . . . Excuse me . . .

She goes out—but lingers on the circle, eavesdropping near the right door. Alan stretches out under his blanket and sleeps. Frank gets up.

FRANK: My wife has romantic ideas, if you receive my meaning.

DYSART: About her family?

FRANK: She thinks she married beneath her. I daresay she did. I don't understand these things myself.

DYSART: Mr Strang, I'm fascinated by the fact that Alan wouldn't ride.

FRANK: Yes, well that's him. He's always been a weird lad,

38

I have to be honest. Can you imagine spending your weekends like that—just cleaning out stalls—with all the things that he could have been doing in the way of Further Education?

DYSART: Except he's hardly a scholar.

FRANK: How do we know? He's never really tried. His mother indulged him. She doesn't care if he can hardly write his own name, and she a school teacher that was. Just as long as he's happy, she says . . .

Dora wrings her hands in anguish.
Frank sits again.

DYSART: Would you say she was closer to him than you are?

FRANK: They've always been thick as thieves. I can't say I entirely approve—especially when I hear her whispering that Bible to him hour after hour, up there in his room.

DYSART: Your wife is religious?

FRANK: Some might say excessively so. Mind you that's her business. But when it comes to dosing it down the boy's throat—well, frankly, he's my son as well as hers. She doesn't see that. Of course, that's the funny thing about religious people. They always think their susceptibilities are more important than non-religious.

DYSART: And you're non-religious, I take it?

FRANK: I'm an atheist, and I don't mind admitting it. If you want my opinion, it's the Bible that's responsible for all this.

DYSART: Why?

FRANK: Well, look at it yourself. A boy spends night after night having this stuff read into him: an innocent man tortured to death—thorns driven into his head—nails into his hands—a spear jammed through his ribs. It can mark anyone for life, that kind of thing. I'm not joking. The boy was absolutely fascinated by all that. He was always mooning over religious pictures. I mean real kinky ones, if you receive my meaning. I had to put a stop to it once or twice! . . . [*pause*] Bloody religion—it's our only real problem in this house, but it's insuperable: I don't mind admitting it.

39

Unable to stand any more, Dora comes in again.

DORA: [*pleasantly*] You must excuse my husband, Doctor. This one subject is something of an obsession with him, isn't it, dear? You must admit.

FRANK: Call it what you like. All that stuff to me is just bad sex.

DORA: And what has that got to do with Alan?

FRANK: Everything! . . . [*seriously*] Everything, Dora!

DORA: I don't understand. What are you saying?

He turns away from her.

DYSART: [*calmingly*] Mr Strang, exactly how informed do you judge your son to *be* about sex?

FRANK: [*tight*] I don't know.

DYSART: You didn't actually instruct him yourself?

FRANK: Not in so many words, no.

DYSART: Did *you*, Mrs Strang?

DORA: Well, I spoke a little, yes. I had to. I've been a teacher, Doctor, and I know what happens if you don't. They find out through magazines and dirty books.

DYSART: What sort of thing did you tell him? I'm sorry if this is embarrassing.

DORA: I told him the biological facts. But I also told him what I believed. That sex is not *just* a biological matter, but spiritual as well. That if God willed, he would fall in love one day. That his task was to prepare himself for the most important happening of his life. And after that, if he was lucky, he might come to know a higher love still . . . I simply . . . don't understand. . . . *Alan!* . . .

She breaks down in sobs.
Her husband gets up and goes to her.

FRANK: [*embarrassed*] There now. There now, Dora. Come on!

DORA: [*with sudden desperation*] All right—laugh! Laugh, as usual!

FRANK: [*kindly*] No one's laughing, Dora.

She glares at him. He puts his arms round her shoulders.

No one's laughing, are they, Doctor?

Tenderly, he leads his wife out of the square, and they resume their places on the bench.
Lights grow much dimmer.

8

A strange noise begins. Alan begins to murmur from his bed. He is having a bad nightmare, moving his hands and body as if frantically straining to tug something back. Dysart leaves the square as the boy's cries increase.

ALAN: Ek!... Ek!... *Ek!...*

Cries of Ek! on tape fill the theatre, from all around.
Dysart reaches the foot of Alan's bed as the boy gives a terrible cry—

EK!

—and wakes up. The sounds snap off. Alan and the Doctor stare at each other. Then abruptly Dysart leaves the area and re-enters the square.

9

Lights grow brighter.
Dysart sits on his bench, left, and opens his file. Alan gets out of bed, leaves his blanket, and comes in. He looks truculent.

DYSART: Hallo. How are you this morning?

Alan stares at him.

Come on: sit down.

Alan crosses the stage and sits on the bench, opposite.

Sorry if I gave you a start last night. I was collecting some papers from my office, and I thought I'd look in on you. Do you dream often?

ALAN: Do *you*?

DYSART: It's my job to ask the questions. Yours to answer them.

ALAN: Says who?

DYSART: Says me. Do you dream often?

ALAN: Do you?

DYSART: Look—Alan.

ALAN: I'll answer if you answer. In turns.

Pause.

DYSART: Very well. Only we have to speak the truth.

ALAN: [*mocking*] Very well.

DYSART: So. Do you dream often?

ALAN: Yes. Do you?

DYSART: Yes. Do you have a special dream?

ALAN: No. Do you?

DYSART: Yes. What was your dream about last night?

ALAN: Can't remember. What's yours about?

DYSART: I said the truth.

ALAN: That is the truth. What's yours about? The special one.

DYSART: Carving up children.

Alan smiles.

My turn!

ALAN: What?

DYSART: What is your first memory of a horse?

ALAN: What d'you mean?

DYSART: The first time one entered your life, in any way.

ALAN: Can't remember.

42

DYSART: Are you sure?

ALAN: Yes.

DYSART: You have no recollection of the first time you noticed a horse?

ALAN: I told you. Now it's my turn. Are you married?

DYSART: [controlling himself] I am.

ALAN: Is she a doctor too?

DYSART: It's my turn.

ALAN: Yes, well what?

DYSART: What is Ek?

Pause.

You shouted it out last night in your sleep. I thought you might like to talk about it.

ALAN: [singing] Double your pleasure,
Double your fun!

DYSART: Come on, now. You can do better than that.

ALAN: [singing louder] With Doublemint, Doublemint Doublemint gum!

DYSART: All right. Good morning.

ALAN: What d'you mean?

DYSART: We're finished for today.

ALAN: But I've only had ten minutes.

DYSART: Too bad.

He picks up a file and studies it.
Alan lingers.

Didn't you hear me? I said, Good morning.

ALAN: That's not fair!

DYSART: No?

ALAN: [savagely] The Government pays you twenty quid an hour to see me. I know. I heard downstairs.

DYSART: Well, go back there and hear some more.

ALAN: *That's not fair!*

He springs up, clenching his fists in a sudden violent rage.

You're a—you're a—You're a swiz! . . . Bloody swiz! . . . Fucking swiz!

DYSART: Do I have to call Nurse?

ALAN: She puts a finger on me, I'll bash her!

DYSART: She'll bash you much harder, I can assure you. Now go away.

He reads his file. Alan stays where he is, emptily clenching his hands. He turns away.
A pause.
A faint hum starts from the Chorus.

ALAN: [*sullenly*] On a beach. . . .

10

He steps out of the square, upstage, and begins to walk round the circle. Warm light glows on it.

DYSART: What?

ALAN: Where I saw a horse. Swizzy.

Lazily he kicks at the sand, and throws stones at the sea.

DYSART: How old were you?

ALAN: How should I know? . . . Six.

DYSART: Well, go on. What were you doing there?

ALAN: Digging.

He throws himself on the ground, downstage centre of the circle, and starts scuffing with his hands.

DYSART: A sandcastle?

ALAN: Well, what else?

DYSART: [*warningly*] And?

ALAN: Suddenly I heard this noise. Coming up behind me.

A young Horseman issues in slow motion out of the tunnel. He carries a riding crop with which he is urging on his

invisible horse, down the right side of the circle.
The hum increases.

DYSART: What noise?
ALAN: Hooves. Splashing.
DYSART: Splashing?
ALAN: The tide was out and he was galloping.
DYSART: Who was?
ALAN: This fellow. Like a college chap. He was on a big
horse—urging him on. I thought he hadn't seen me. I
called out: Hey!

*The Horseman goes into natural time, charging fast round
the downstage corner of the square straight at Alan.*

and they just swerved in time!
HORSEMAN: [*reining back*] Whoa! . . . Whoa there! *Whoa!*
. . . Sorry! I didn't see you! . . . Did I scare you?
ALAN: No!
HORSEMAN: [*looking down on him*] That's a terrific castle!
ALAN: What's his name?
HORSEMAN: Trojan. You can stroke him, if you like. He
won't mind.

*Shyly Alan stretches up on tip-toe, and pats an invisible
shoulder.*

[*amused*] You can hardly reach down there. Would you
like to come up?

Alan nods, eyes wide.

All right. Come round this side. You always mount a
horse from the left. I'll give you a lift. O.K.?

Alan goes round on the other side.

Here we go, now. Just do nothing. Upsadaisy!

*Alan sets his foot on the Horseman's thigh, and is lifted by
him up on to his shoulders.*

45

The hum from the Chorus becomes exultant. Then stops.

All right?

Alan nods.

Good. Now all you do is hold onto his mane.

He holds up the crop, and Alan grips on to it.

Tight now. And grip with your knees. All right?
All set? . . . Come on, then, Trojan. Let's go!

The Horseman walks slowly upstage round the circle, with Alan's legs tight round his neck.

DYSART: How was it? Was it wonderful?

Alan rides in silence.

Can't you remember?
HORSEMAN: Do you want to go faster?
ALAN: Yes!
HORSEMAN: O.K. All you have to do is say 'Come on, Trojan—bear me away!' . . . Say it, then!
ALAN: Bear me away!

The Horseman starts to run with Alan round the circle.

DYSART: You went fast?
ALAN: Yes!
DYSART: Weren't you frightened?
ALAN: No!
HORSEMAN: Come on now, Trojan! Bear us away! Hold on! Come on now! . . .

He runs faster. Alan begins to laugh. Then suddenly, as they reach again the right downstage corner, Frank and Dora stand up in alarm.

DORA: Alan!

FRANK: Alan!
DORA: Alan, stop!

Frank runs round after them. Dora follows behind.

FRANK: Hey, you! *You!* . . .
HORSEMAN: Whoa, boy! . . . Whoa! . . .

*He reins the horse round, and wheels to face the parents.
This all goes fast.*

FRANK: What do you imagine you are doing?
HORSEMAN: [*ironic*] 'Imagine'?
FRANK: What is my son doing up there?

HORSEMAN: Water-skiing!

Dora joins them, breathless.

DORA: Is he all right, Frank? . . . He's not hurt?
FRANK: Don't you think you should ask permission before
   doing a stupid thing like that?
HORSEMAN: What's stupid?
ALAN: It's lovely, dad!
DORA: Alan, come down here!
HORSEMAN: The boy's perfectly safe. Please don't be
   hysterical.
FRANK: Don't you be la-di-da with me, young man! Come
   down here, Alan. You heard what your mother said.
ALAN: No.
FRANK: Come down at once. Right this moment.
ALAN: No . . . NO!
FRANK: [*in a fury*] I said—this moment!

*He pulls Alan from the Horseman's shoulders. The boy
   shrieks, and falls to the ground.*

HORSEMAN: Watch it!
DORA: Frank!

She runs to her son, and kneels. The Horseman skitters.

HORSEMAN: Are you mad? D'you want to terrify the horse?
DORA: He's grazed his knee. Frank—the boy's hurt!
ALAN: I'm not! I'm *not!*
FRANK: What's your name?
HORSEMAN: Jesse James.
DORA: Frank, he's bleeding!
FRANK: I intend to report you to the police for endanger-
    ing the lives of children.
HORSEMAN: Go right ahead!
DORA: Can you stand, dear?
ALAN: Oh, *stop* it! . . .
FRANK: You're a public menace, d'you know that? How
    dare you pick up children and put them on dangerous
    animals.
HORSEMAN: Dangerous?
FRANK: Of course dangerous. Look at his eyes. They're
    rolling.
HORSEMAN: So are yours!
FRANK: In my opinion that is a dangerous animal. In my
    considered opinion you are both dangers to the safety of
    this beach.
HORSEMAN: And in my opinion, you're a stupid fart!
DORA: Frank, leave it!
FRANK: What did you say?
DORA: It's not important, Frank—really!
FRANK: *What did you say?*
HORSEMAN: Oh bugger off! Sorry, chum! Come on, Trojan!

*He urges his horse straight at them, then wheels it and
gallops off round the right side of the circle and away up
the tunnel, out of sight. The parents cry out, as they are
covered with sand and water. Frank runs after him, and
round the left side of the circle, with his wife following
after.*

ALAN: Splash, splash, splash! All three of us got covered
    with water! Dad got absolutely soaked!
FRANK: [*shouting after the Horseman*] Hooligan! Filthy
    hooligan!
ALAN: I wanted to laugh!
FRANK: Upper class riff-raff! That's all they are, people who

go riding! That's what they *want*—trample on ordinary people!

DORA: Don't be absurd, Frank.

FRANK: It's why they do it. It's why they bloody do it!

DORA: [*amused*] Look at you. You're covered!

FRANK: Not as much as you. There's sand all over your hair!

She starts to laugh.

[*shouting*] Hooligan! Bloody hooligan!

She starts to laugh more. He tries to brush the sand out of her hair.

What are you laughing at? It's not funny. It's not funny at all, Dora!

She goes off, right, still laughing. Alan edges into the square, still on the ground.

It's just not funny! . . .

Frank returns to his place on the beach, sulky.
Abrupt silence.

ALAN: And that's all I remember.

DYSART: And a lot, too. Thank you . . . You know, I've never been on a horse in my life.

ALAN: [*not looking at him*] Nor me.

DYSART: You mean, after that?

ALAN: Yes.

DYSART: But you must have done at the stables?

ALAN: No.

DYSART: Never?

ALAN: No.

DYSART: How come?

ALAN: I didn't care to.

DYSART: Did it have anything to do with falling off like that, all those years ago?

ALAN: [*tight*] I just didn't care to, that's all.

49

DYSART: Do you think of that scene often?

ALAN: I suppose.

DYSART: Why, do you think?

ALAN: 'Cos it's funny.

DYSART: Is that all?

ALAN: What else? My turn. . . . I told you a secret: now you tell me one.

DYSART: All right. I have patients who've got things to tell me, only they're ashamed to say them to my face. What do you think I do about that?

ALAN: What?

DYSART: I give them this little tape recorder.

He takes a small tape recorder and microphone from his pocket.

They go off to another room, and send me the tape through Nurse. They don't have to listen to it with me.

ALAN: That's stupid.

DYSART: All you do is press this button, and speak into this. It's very simple. Anyway, your time's up for today. I'll see you tomorrow.

ALAN: [*getting up*] Maybe.

DYSART: Maybe?

ALAN: If I feel like it.

He is about to go out. Then suddenly he returns to Dysart and takes the machine from him.

It's stupid.

He leaves the square and goes back to his bed.

11

DORA: [*calling out*] Doctor!

Dora re-enters and comes straight on to the square from

*the right. She wears an overcoat, and is nervously carrying
a shopping bag.*

DYSART: That same evening, his mother appeared.

DORA: Hallo, Doctor.

DYSART: Mrs Strang!

DORA: I've been shopping in the neighbourhood. I thought I
might just look in.

DYSART: Did you want to see Alan?

DORA: [*uncomfortably*] No, no . . . Not just at the moment.
Actually, it's more you I wanted to see.

DYSART: Yes?

DORA: You see, there's something Mr Strang and I thought
you ought to know. We discussed it, and it might just
be important.

DYSART: Well, come and sit down.

DORA: I can't stay more than a moment. I'm late as it is.
Mr Strang will be wanting his dinner.

DYSART: Ah. [*encouragingly*] So, what was it you wanted to
tell me?

She sits on the upstage bench.

DORA: Well, do you remember that photograph I men-
tioned to you. The one Mr Strang gave Alan to decorate
his bedroom a few years ago?

DYSART: Yes. A horse looking over a gate, wasn't it?

DORA: That's right. Well, actually, it took the place of
another kind of picture altogether.

DYSART: What kind?

DORA: It was a reproduction of Our Lord on his way to
Calvary. Alan found it in Reeds Art Shop, and fell
absolutely in love with it. He insisted on buying it with
his pocket money, and hanging it at the foot of his bed
where he could see it last thing at night. My husband
was very displeased.

DYSART: Because it was religious?

DORA: In all fairness I must admit it was a little extreme.
The Christ was loaded down with chains, and the cen-
turions were really laying on the stripes. It certainly
would not have been my choice, but I don't believe in

51

interfering too much with children, so I said nothing.

DYSART: But Mr Strang did?

DORA: He stood it for a while, but one day we had one of our tiffs about religion, and he went straight upstairs, tore it off the boy's wall and threw it in the dustbin. Alan went quite hysterical. He cried for days without stopping —and he was not a crier, you know.

DYSART: But he recovered when he was given the photograph of the horse in its place?

DORA: He certainly seemed to. At least, he hung it in exactly the same position, and we had no more of that awful weeping.

DYSART: Thank you, Mrs Strang. That *is* interesting . . . Exactly how long ago was that? Can you remember?

DORA: It must be five years ago, Doctor. Alan would have been about twelve. How is he, by the way?

DYSART: Bearing up.

She rises.

DORA: Please give him my love.

DYSART: You can see him any time you want, you know.

DORA: Perhaps if I could come one afternoon without Mr Strang. He and Alan don't exactly get on at the moment, as you can imagine.

DYSART: Whatever you decide, Mrs Strang . . . Oh, one thing.

DORA: Yes?

DYSART: Could you describe that photograph of the horse in a litle more detail for me? I presume it's still in his bedroom?

DORA: Oh, yes. It's a most remarkable picture, really. You very rarely see a horse taken from that angle—absolutely head on. That's what makes it so interesting.

DYSART: Why? What does it look like?

DORA: Well, it's most extraordinary. It comes out all eyes.

DYSART: Staring straight at you?

DORA: Yes, that's right . . .

An uncomfortable pause.

I'll come and see him one day very soon, Doctor. Good-bye.

She leaves, and resumes her place by her husband.

DYSART: [*to audience*] It was then— that moment—I felt real alarm. What was it? The shadow of a giant head across my desk? . . . At any rate, the feeling got worse with the stable-owner's visit.

12

Dalton comes in to the square: heavy-set: mid-fifties.

DALTON: Dr Dysart?
DYSART: Mr Dalton. It's very good of you to come.
DALTON: It is, actually. In my opinion the boy should be in prison. Not in a hospital at the tax-payers' expense.
DYSART: Please sit down.

Dalton sits.

This must have been a terrible experience for you.
DALTON: Terrible? I don't think I'll ever get over it. Jill's had a nervous breakdown.
DYSART: Jill?
DALTON: The girl who worked for me. Of course, she feels responsible in a way. Being the one who introduced him in the first place.
DYSART: He was introduced to the stable by a girl?
DALTON: Jill Mason. He met her somewhere, and asked for a job. She told him to come and see me. I wish to Christ she never had.
DYSART: But when he first appeared he didn't seem in any way peculiar?
DALTON: No, he was bloody good. He'd spend hours with the horses cleaning and grooming them, way over the call of duty. I thought he was a real find.

DYSART: Apparently, during the whole time he worked for you, he never actually rode.

DALTON: That's true.

DYSART: Wasn't that peculiar?

DALTON: Very . . . *If* he didn't.

DYSART: What do you mean?

Dalton rises.

DALTON: Because on and off, that whole year, I had the feeling the horses were being taken out at night.

DYSART: At night?

DALTON: There were just odd things I noticed. I mean too often one or other of them would be sweaty first thing in the morning, when it wasn't sick. Very sweaty, too. And its stall wouldn't be near as mucky as it should be if it had been in all night. I never paid it much mind at the time. It was only when I realised I'd been hiring a loony, I came to wonder if he hadn't been riding all the time, behind our backs.

DYSART: But wouldn't you have noticed if things had been disturbed?

DALTON: Nothing ever was. Still, he's a neat worker. That wouldn't prove anything.

DYSART: Aren't the stables locked at night?

DALTON: Yes.

DYSART: And someone sleeps on the premises?

DALTON: Me and my son.

DYSART: Two people?

DALTON: I'm sorry, Doctor. It's obviously just my fancy. I tell you, this thing has shaken me so bad, I'm liable to believe anything. If there's nothing else, I'll be going.

DYSART: Look: even if you were right, why should anyone do that? Why would any boy prefer to ride by himself at night, when he could go off with others during the day.

DALTON: Are you asking me? He's a loony, isn't he?

Dalton leaves the square and sits again in his place. Dysart watches him go.

ALAN: It was *sexy*.
DYSART: His tape arrived that evening.

13

Alan is sitting on his bed holding the tape-recorder. Nurse approaches briskly, takes the machine from him—gives it to Dysart in the square—and leaves again, resuming her seat. Dysart switches on the tape.

ALAN: That's what you want to know, isn't it? All right: it was. I'm talking about the beach. That time when I was a kid. What I told you about. . . .

Pause. He is in great emotional difficulty.
Dysart sits on the left bench listening, file in hand. Alan rises and stands directly behind him, but on the circle, as if recording the ensuing speech. He never, of course, looks directly at the Doctor.

I was pushed forward on the horse. There was sweat on my legs from his neck. The fellow held me tight, and let me turn the horse which way I wanted. All that power going any way you wanted . . . His sides were all warm, and the smell . . . Then suddenly I was on the ground, where Dad pulled me. I could have bashed him . . .

Pause.

Something else. When the horse first appeared, I looked up into his mouth. It was huge. There was this chain in it. The fellow pulled it, and cream dripped out. I said 'Does it hurt?' And he said—the horse said—said—

He stops, in anguish. Dysart makes a note in his file.

[*desperately*] It was always the same, after that. Every time I heard one clop by, I had to run and see. Up a country lane or anywhere. They sort of pulled me. I couldn't take my eyes off them. Just to watch their skins. The way their necks twist, and sweat shines in the folds . . . [*pause*] I can't remember when it started. Mum reading to me about Prince who no one could ride, except one boy. Or the white horse in Revelations. 'He that sat upon him was called Faithful and True. His eyes were as flames of fire, and he had a name written that no man knew but himself' . . . Words like reins. Stirrup. Flanks . . . 'Dashing his spurs against his charger's flanks!' . . . Even the words made me feel— . . . Years, I never told anyone. Mum wouldn't understand. She likes Equitation'. Bowler hats and jodhpurs! 'My grandfather dressed for the horse,' she says. What does that mean? The horse isn't dressed. It's the most naked thing you ever saw! More than a dog or a cat or anything. Even the most broken down old nag has got its *life!* To put a bowler on it is *filthy!* . . . Putting them through their paces! Bloody gymkhanas! . . . No one understands! . . . Except cowboys. They do. I wish I was a cowboy. They're free. They just swing up and then it's miles of grass . . . I bet all cowboys are *orphans!* . . . I bet they are!

NURSE: Mr Strang to see you, Doctor.

DYSART: [*in surprise*] Mr Strang? Show him up, please.

ALAN: No one ever says to cowboys 'Receive my meaning'! They wouldn't dare. Or 'God' all the time. [*mimicking his mother*] 'God sees you, Alan. God's got eyes everywhere—'

He stops abruptly.

I'm not doing any more! . . . I hate this! . . . You can whistle for anymore. I've had it!

He returns angrily to his bed, throwing the blanket over him.
Dysart switches off the tape.

14

*Frank Strang comes into the square, his hat in his hand.
He is nervous and embarrassed.*

DYSART: [*welcoming*] Hallo, Mr Strang.

FRANK: I was just passing. I hope it's not too late.

DYSART: Of course not. I'm delighted to see you.

FRANK: My wife doesn't know I'm here. I'd be grateful to
you if you didn't enlighten her, if you receive my meaning.

DYSART: Everything that happens in this room is confidential, Mr Strang.

FRANK: I hope so . . . I hope so . . .

DYSART: [*gently*] Do you have something to tell me?

FRANK: As a matter of fact I have. Yes.

DYSART: Your wife told me about the photograph.

FRANK: I know, it's not that! It's *about* that, but it's—
worse. . . . I wanted to tell you the other night, but I
couldn't in front of Dora. Maybe I should have. It might
show her where all that stuff leads to, she drills into
the boy behind my back.

DYSART: What kind of thing is it?

FRANK: Something I witnessed.

DYSART: Where?

FRANK: At home. About eighteen months ago.

DYSART: Go on.

FRANK: It was late. I'd gone upstairs to fetch something.
The boy had been in bed hours, or so I thought.

DYSART: Go on.

FRANK: As I came along the passage I saw the door of his
bedroom was ajar. I'm sure he didn't know it was.
From inside I heard the sound of this chanting.

DYSART: Chanting?

FRANK: Like the Bible. One of those lists his mother's
always reading to him.

DYSART: What kind of list?

FRANK: Those Begats. So-and-so begat, you know. Gene-
alogy.

DYSART: Can you remember what Alan's list sounded like?

FRANK: Well, the *sort* of thing. I stood there absolutely
astonished. The first word I heard was . . .

ALAN: [*rising and chanting*] Prince!

DYSART: Prince?

FRANK: Prince begat Prance. That sort of nonsense.

Alan moves slowly to the center of the circle, downstage.

ALAN: And Prance begat Prankus! And Prankus begat
Flankus!

FRANK: I looked through the door, and he was standing in
the moonlight in his pyjamas, right in front of that big
photograph.

DYSART: The horse with the huge eyes?

FRANK: Right.

ALAN: Flankus begat Spankus. And Spankus begat Spunkus
the Great, who lived three score years!

FRANK: It was all like that. I can't remember the exact
names, of course. Then suddenly he knelt down.

DYSART: In front of the photograph?

FRANK: Yes. Right there at the foot of his bed.

ALAN: [*kneeling*] And Legwus begat Neckwus. And Neckwus begat Fleckwus, the King of Spit. And Fleckwus
spoke out of his chinkle-chankle!

He bows himself to the ground.

DYSART: What?

FRANK: I'm sure that was the word. I've never forgotten it.
Chinkle-chankle.

Alan raises his head and extends his hands up in glory.

ALAN: And he said 'Behold—I give you Equus, my only
begotten son!'

DYSART: Equus?

FRANK: Yes. No doubt of that. He repeated that word
several times. 'Equus my only begotten son."

ALAN: [*reverently*] Ek . . . . wus!

DYSART: [*suddenly understanding: almost 'aside'*] *Ek* . . . .
Ek . . . .

FRANK: [*embarrassed*] And then . . .

DYSART: Yes: what?

FRANK: He took a piece of string out of his pocket. Made
up into a noose. And put it in his mouth.

Alan bridles himself with invisible string, and pulls it back.

And then with his other hand he picked up a coat
hanger. A wooden coat hanger, and—and—

DYSART: Began to beat himself?

*Alan, in mime, begins to thrash himself, increasing the
strokes in speed and viciousness.*
Pause.

FRANK: You see why I couldn't tell his mother. . . . Religion. Religion's at the bottom of all this!

DYSART: What did you do?

FRANK: Nothing. I coughed—and went back downstairs.

*The boy starts guiltily—tears the string from his mouth—
and scrambles back to bed.*

DYSART: Did you ever speak to him about it later? Even
obliquely?

FRANK: [*unhappily*] I can't speak of things like that,
Doctor. It's not in my nature.

DYSART: [*kindly*] No. I see that.

FRANK: But I thought you ought to know. So I came.

DYSART: [*warmly*] Yes. I'm very grateful to you. Thank
you.

Pause.

FRANK: Well, that's it . . .

DYSART: Is there anything else?

FRANK: [*even more embarrassed*] There is actually. One
thing.

DYSART: What's that?

FRANK: On the night that he did it—that awful thing in the stable—

DYSART: Yes?

FRANK: That very night, he was out with a girl.

DYSART: How d'you know that?

FRANK: I just know.

DYSART: [*puzzled*] Did he tell you?

FRANK: I can't say any more.

DYSART: I don't quite understand.

FRANK: Everything said in here is confidential, you said.

DYSART: Absolutely.

FRANK: Then ask him. Ask him about taking a girl out, that very night he did it. . . . [*abruptly*] Goodbye, Doctor.

He goes. Dysart looks after him.
Frank resumes his seat.

15

Alan gets up and enters the square.

DYSART: Alan! Come in. Sit down. [*pleasantly*] What did you do last night?

ALAN: Watched telly.

DYSART: Any good?

ALAN: All right.

DYSART: Thanks for the tape. It was excellent.

ALAN: I'm not making any more.

DYSART: One thing I didn't quite understand. You began to say something about the horse on the beach talking to you.

ALAN: That's stupid. Horses don't talk.

DYSART: So I believe.

ALAN: I don't know what you mean.

DYSART: Never mind. Tell me something else. Who introduced you to the stable to begin with?

Pause.

ALAN: Someone I met.

DYSART: Where?

ALAN: Bryson's.

DYSART: The shop where you worked?

ALAN: Yes.

DYSART: That's a funny place for you to be. Whose idea was that?

ALAN: Dad.

DYSART: I'd have thought he'd have wanted you to work with him.

ALAN: I haven't the aptitude. And printing's a failing trade. If you receive my meaning.

DYSART: [*amused*] I see . . . What did your mother think?

ALAN: Shops are common.

DYSART: And you?

ALAN: I loved it.

DYSART: Really?

ALAN: [*sarcastic*] Why not? You get to spend every minute with electrical things. It's fun.

Nurse, Dalton and the actors playing horses call out to him as Customers, seated where they are. Their voices are aggressive and demanding. There is a constant background mumbling, made up of trade names, out of which can clearly be distinguished the italicized words, which are shouted out.

CUSTOMER: *Philco!*

ALAN: [*to Dysart*] Of course it might just drive you off your chump.

CUSTOMER: I want to buy a hot-plate. I'm told the *Philco* is a good make!

ALAN: I think it is, madam.

CUSTOMER: Remington ladies' shavers?

ALAN: I'm not sure, madam.

CUSTOMER: *Robex* tableware?

CUSTOMER: *Croydex?*

CUSTOMER: *Volex?*

CUSTOMER: *Pifco* automatic toothbrushes?

61

ALAN: I'll find out, sir.
CUSTOMER: Beautiflor!
CUSTOMER: Windowlene!
CUSTOMER: I want a *Philco* transistor radio!
CUSTOMER: This isn't a *Remington!* I wanted a *Remington!*
ALAN: Sorry.
CUSTOMER: Are you a dealer for *Hoover?*
ALAN: Sorry.
CUSTOMER: I wanted the heat retaining *Pifco!*
ALAN: *Sorry!*

Jill comes into the square; a girl in her early twenties, pretty and middle class. She wears a sweater and jeans. The mumbling stops.

JILL: Hallo.
ALAN: Hallo.
JILL: Have you any blades for a clipping machine?
JILL: Clipping?
JILL: To clip horses.

Pause. He stares at her, open-mouthed.

What's the matter?
ALAN: You work at Dalton's stables. I've seen you.

During the following, he mimes putting away a pile of boxes on a shelf in the shop.

JILL: I've seen you too, haven't I? You're the boy who's always staring into the yard around lunch-time.
ALAN: Me?
JILL: You're there most days.
ALAN: Not me.
JILL: [*amused*] Of course it's you. Mr. Dalton was only saying the other day: 'Who's that boy keeps staring in at the door?' Are you looking for a job or something?
ALAN: [*eagerly*] Is there one?
JILL: I don't know.
ALAN: I can only do weekends.

JILL: That's when most people ride. We can always use extra hands. It'd mainly be mucking out.
ALAN: I don't mind.
JILL: Can you ride?
ALAN: No . . . No . . . I don't want to.

She looks at him curiously.

Please.
JILL: Come up on Saturday. I'll introduce you to Mr Dalton.

She leaves the square.

DYSART: When was this? About a year ago?
ALAN: I suppose.
DYSART: And she did?
ALAN: Yes.

Briskly he moves the three benches to form three stalls in the stable.

16

Rich light falls on the square.
An exultant humming from the Chorus.
Tramping is heard. Three actors playing horses rise from their places. Together they unhook three horse masks from the ladders to left and right, put them on with rigid timing, and walk with swaying horse-motion into the square. Their metal hooves stamp on the wood. Their masks turn and toss high above their heads—as they will do sporadically throughout all horse scenes—making the steel gleam in the light.
For a moment they seem to converge on the boy as he stands in the middle of the stable, but then they swiftly turn and take up positions as if tethered by the head, with their invisible rumps towards him, one by each bench.

Alan is sunk in this glowing world of horses. Lost in wonder, he starts almost involuntarily to kneel on the floor in reverence—but is sharply interrupted by the cheery voice of Dalton, coming into the stable, followed by Jill. The boy straightens up guiltily.

DALTON: First thing to learn is drill. Learn it and keep to it. I want this place neat, dry and clean at all times. After you've mucked out, Jill will show you some grooming. What we call strapping a horse.
JILL: I think Trooper's got a stone.
DALTON: Yes? Let's see.

He crosses to the horse by the left bench, who is balancing one hoof on its tip. He picks up the hoof.

You're right. [*to Alan*] See this? This V here. It's what's called a frog. Sort of shock-absorber. Once you pierce that, it takes ages to heal—so you want to watch for it. You clean it out with this. What we call a hoof-pick.

He takes from his pocket an invisible pick.

Mind how you go with it. It's very sharp. Use it like this.

He quickly takes the stone out.

See?

Alan nods, fascinated.

You'll soon get the hang of it. Jill will look after you. What she doesn't know about stables, isn't worth knowing.
JILL: [*pleased*] Oh yes, I'm sure!
DALTON: [*handing Alan the pick*] Careful how you go with that. The main rule is: anything you don't know—ask. Never pretend you know something when you don't. [*smiling*] Actually, the main rule is: enjoy yourself. All right?

ALAN: Yes, sir.
DALTON: Good lad. See you later.

He nods to them cheerfully, and leaves the square. Alan clearly puts the invisible hoof-pick on the rail, downstage left.

JILL: All right, let's start on some grooming. Why don't we begin with him? He looks as if he needs it.

They approach Nugget, who is standing to the right. She pats him. Alan sits and watches her.

This is Nugget. He's my favorite. He's as gentle as a baby, aren't you? But terribly fast if you want him to be.

During the following, she mimes both the actions and the objects, which she picks up from the right bench.

Now this is the dandy, and we start with that. Then you move on to the body brush. This is the most important, and you use it with this curry-comb. Now you always groom the same way: from the ears downward. Don't be afraid to do it hard. The harder you do it, the more the horse loves it. Push it right through the coat: like this.

The boy watches in fascination as she brushes the invisible body of Nugget, scraping the dirt and hair off on to the invisible curry-comb. Now and then the horse mask moves very slightly in pleasure.

Down towards the tail and right through the coat. See how he loves it? I'm giving you a lovely massage, boy, aren't I? . . . You try.

She hands him the brush. Gingerly he rises and approaches Nugget. Embarrassed and excited, he copies her movements, inexpertly.

Keep it nice and easy. Never rush. Down towards the

tail and right through the coat. That's it. Again. Down
towards the tail and right through the coat. . . . Very
good. Now you keep that up for fifteen minutes and
then do old Trooper. Will you?

Alan nods.

You've got a feel for it. I can tell. It's going to be nice
teaching you. See you later.

She leaves the square and resumes her place.
Alan is left alone with the horses.
They all stamp. He approaches Nugget again, and touches
the horse's shoulder. The mask turns sharply in his direc-
tion. The boy pauses, then moves his hand gently over the
outline of the neck and back. The mask is re-assured. It
stares ahead unmoving. Then Alan lifts his palm to his
face and smells it deeply, closing his eyes.
Dysart rise from his bench, and begins to walk slowly
upstage round the circle.

DYSART: Was that good? Touching them.

Alan gives a faint groan.

ALAN: Mmm.
DYSART: It must have been marvelous, being near them at
last . . . Stroking them . . . Making them fresh and glossy
. . . Tell me . . .

Silence. Alan begins to brush Nugget.

How about the girl? Did you like her?
ALAN: [*tight*] All right.
DYSART: Just all right?

Alan changes his position, moving round Nugget's rump so
that his back is to the audience. He brushes harder. Dysart
comes downstage around the circle, and finally back to
his bench.

66

Was she friendly?

ALAN: Yes.

DYSART: Or stand-offish?

ALAN: Yes.

DYSART: Well which?

ALAN: What?

DYSART: Which was she?

Alan brushes harder.

Did you take her out? Come on now: tell me. Did you
have a date with her?

ALAN: What?

DYSART: [*sitting*] Tell me if you did.

The boy suddenly explodes in one of his rages.

ALAN: [*yelling*] TELL ME!

All the masks toss at the noise.

DYSART: What?

ALAN: *Tell me, tell me, tell me, tell me!*

*Alan storms out of the square, and downstage to where
Dysart sits. He is raging. During the ensuing, the horses
leave by all three openings.*

On and on, sitting there! Nosey Parker! That's all you
are! Bloody Nosey Parker! Just like Dad. On and on and
bloody on! Tell me, tell me, tell me! . . . Answer this.
Answer that. Never stop!—

*He marches round the circle and back into the square.
Dysart rises and enters it from the other side.*

17

Lights brighten.

DYSART: I'm sorry.

Alan slams about what is now the office again, replacing the benches to their usual position.

ALAN: All right, it's my turn now. You tell me! Answer me!
DYSART: We're not playing that game now.
ALAN: We're playing what I say.
DYSART: All right. What do you want to know?

He sits.

ALAN: Do *you* have dates?
DYSART: I told you. I'm married.

Alan approaches him, very hostile.

ALAN: I know. Her name's Margaret. She's a dentist! You see, I found out! What made you go with her? Did you use to bite her hands when she did you in the chair?

The boy sits next to him, close.

DYSART: That's not very funny.
ALAN: Do you have girls behind her back?
DYSART: No.
ALAN: Then what? Do you fuck her?
DYSART: That's enough now.

He rises and moves away.

ALAN: Come on, tell me! Tell me, tell me!
DYSART: I said that's enough now.

Alan rises too and walks around him.

I bet you don't. I bet you never touch her. Come on, tell me. You've got no kids, have you? Is that because you don't fuck?
DYSART: [*sharp*] Go to your room. Go on: quick march.

Pause. Alan moves away from him, insolently takes up a packet of Dysart's cigarettes from the bench, and extracts one.

Give me those cigarettes.

The boy puts one in his mouth.

[*exploding*] Alan, *give them to me!*

Reluctantly Alan shoves the cigarette back in the packet, turns and hands it to him.

Now go!

Alan bolts out of the square, and back to his bed. Dysart, unnerved, addresses the audience.

Brilliant! Absolutely brilliant! The boy's on the run, so he gets defensive. What am *I*, then? . . . Wicked little bastard—he knew exactly what questions to try. He'd actually marched himself round the hospital, making enquiries about my wife. Wicked and—of course, perceptive. Every since I made that crack about carving up children, he's been aware of me in an absolutely specific way. Of course, there's nothing novel in that. Advanced neurotics can be dazzling at that game. They aim unswervingly at your area of maximum vulnerability . . . Which I suppose is as good a way as any of describing Margaret.

He sits. Hesther enters the square.
Light grows warmer.

18

HESTHER: Now stop it.
DYSART: Do I embarrass you?
HESTHER: I suspect you're about to.

Pause.

DYSART: My wife doesn't understand me, Your Honour.
HESTHER: Do you understand her?
DYSART: No. Obviously I never did.
HESTHER: I'm sorry. I've never liked to ask but I've always imagined you weren't exactly compatible.

She moves to sit opposite.

DYSART: We were. It actually worked for a bit. I mean for both of us. We worked for each other, She actually for me through a kind of briskness. A clear, red-headed, inaccessible briskness which kept me keyed up for months. Mind you, if you're kinky for Northern Hygenic, as I am, you can't find anything much more compelling than a Scottish Lady Dentist.
HESTHER: It's *you* who are wicked, you know!
DYSART: Not at all: She got exactly the same from me. Antiseptic proficiency. I was like that in those days. We suited each other admirably. I see us in our wedding photo: Doctor and Doctor Mac Brisk. We were brisk in our wooing, brisk in our wedding, brisk in our disappointment. We turned from each other briskly into our separate surgeries: and now there's damn all.
HESTHER: You have no children, have you?
DYSART: No, we didn't go in for them. Instead, she sits beside our salmon-pink, glazed brick fireplace, and knits things for orphans in a home she helps with. And I sit opposite, turning the pages of art books on Ancient Greece. Occasionally, I still trail a faint scent of my

enthusiasm across her path. I pass her a picture of the sacred acrobats of Crete leaping through the horns of running bulls—and she'll say: 'Och, Martin. what an *absurred* thing to be doing! The Highland Games, now there's *norrmal sport!*' Or she'll observe, just after I've told her a story from the Iliad: 'You know, when you come to think of it, Agamemnon and that lot were nothing but a bunch of ruffians from the Gorbals, only with fancy names!' [*He rises*] You get the picture. She's turned into a Shrink. The familiar domestic monster. Margaret Dysart: the Shrink's Shrink.

HESTHER: That's cruel, Martin.

DYSART: Yes. Do you know what it's like for two people to live in the same house as if they were in different parts of the world? Mentally, she's always in some drizzly kirk of her own inheriting: and I'm in some Doric temple—clouds tearing through pillars—eagles bearing prophecies out of the sky. She finds all that repulsive. All my wife has ever taken from the Mediterranean— from that whole vast intuitive culture—are four bottles of Chianti to make into lamps, and two china condiment donkeys labelled Sally and Peppy.

Pause.

[*more intimately*] I wish there was one person in my life I could show. One instinctive, absolutely unbrisk person I could take to Greece, and stand in front of certain shrines and sacred streams and say 'Look! Life is only comprehensible through a thousand local Gods. And not just the old dead ones with names like Zeus—no, but living Geniuses of Place and Person! And not just Greece but modern England! Spirits of certain trees, certain curves of brick wall, certain chip shops, if you like, and slate roofs—just as of certain frowns in people and slouches . . . I'd say to them—'Worship as many as you can see—and more will appear!' . . . If I had a son, I bet you he'd come out exactly like his mother. Utterly worshipless. Would you like a drink?

HESTHER: No, thanks. Actually, I've got to be going. As usual . . .

DYSART: Really?

HESTHER: Really. I've got an Everest of papers to get through before bed.

DYSART: You never stop, do you?

HESTHER: Do you?

DYSART: This boy, with his stare. He's trying to save himself through me.

HESTHER: I'd say so.

DYSART: What am I trying to do to him?

HESTHER: Restore him, surely?

DYSART: To what?

HESTHER: A normal life.

DYSART: Normal?

HESTHER: It still means something.

DYSART: Does it?

HESTHER: Of course.

DYSART: You mean a normal boy has one head: a normal head has two ears?

HESTHER: You know I don't.

DYSART: Then what else?

HESTHER: [*lightly*] Oh, stop it.

DYSART: No, what? You tell me.

HESTHER: [*rising: smiling*] I won't be put on the stand like this, Martin. You're really disgraceful! . . . [*Pause*] You know what I mean by a normal smile in a child's eyes, and one that isn't—even if I can't exactly define it. Don't you?

DYSART: Yes.

HESTHER: Then we have a duty to that, surely? Both of us.

DYSART: Touché. . . . I'll talk to you.

HESTHER: Dismissed?

DYSART: You said you had to go.

HESTHER: I do . . . [*she kisses his cheek*]. Thank you for what you're doing. . . . You're going through a rotten patch at the moment. I'm sorry . . . I suppose one of the few things one can do is simply hold on to priorities.

DYSART: Like what?

HESTHER: Oh—children before grown-ups. Things like that.

He contemplates her.

DYSART: You're really quite splendid.
HESTHER: Famous for it. Goodnight.

She leaves him.

DYSART: [*to himself—or to the audience*] Normal! . . .
Normal!

19

Alan rises and enters the square. He is subdued.

DYSART: Good afternoon.
ALAN: Afternoon.
DYSART: I'm sorry about our row yesterday.
ALAN: It was stupid.
DYSART: It was.
ALAN: What I said, I mean.
DYSART: How are you sleeping?

Alan shrugs.

You're not feeling well, are you?
ALAN: All right.
DYSART: Would you like to play a game? It could make
you feel better.
ALAN: What kind?
DYSART: It's called *Blink*. You have to fix your eyes on
something: say, that little stain over there on the wall—
and I tap this pen on the desk. The first time I tap it,
you close your eyes. The next time you open them. And
so on. Close, open, close, open, till I say Stop.
ALAN: How can that make you feel better?
DYSART: It relaxes you. You'll feel as though you're talking
to me in your sleep.
ALAN: It's stupid.

DYSART: You don't have to do it, if you don't want to.

ALAN: I didn't say I didn't want to.

DYSART: Well?

ALAN: I don't mind.

DYSART: Good. Sit down and start watching that stain. Put your hands by your sides, and open the fingers wide.

He opens the left bench and Alan sits on the end of it.

The thing is to feel comfortable, and relax absolutely . . . Are you looking at the stain?

ALAN: Yes.

DYSART: Right. Now try and keep your mind as blank as possible.

ALAN: That's not difficult.

DYSART: Ssh. Stop talking . . . On the first tap, close. On the second, open. Are you ready?

Alan nods. Dysart taps his pen on the wooden rail. Alan shuts his eyes. Dysart taps again. Alan opens them. The taps are evenly spaced. After four of them the sound cuts out, and is replaced by a louder, metallic sound, on tape. Dysart talks through this, to the audience—the light changes to cold—while the boy sits in front of him, staring at the wall, opening and shutting his eyes.

The Normal is the good smile in a child's eyes—all right. It is also the dead stare in a million adults. It both sustains and kills—like a God. It is the Ordinary made beautiful: it is also the Average made lethal. The Normal is the indispensable, murderous God of Health, and I am his Priest. My tools are very delicate. My compassion is honest. I have honestly assisted children in this room. I have talked away terrors and relieved many agonies. But also—beyond question—I have cut from them parts of individuality repugnant to this God, in both his aspects. Parts sacred to rarer and more wonderful Gods. And at what length . . . Sacrifices to Zeus took at the most surely, sixty seconds each. Sacrifices to the Normal can take as long as sixty months.

74

The natural sound of the pencil resumes.
Light changes back.

[*to Alan*] Now your eyes are feeling heavy. You want
to sleep, don't you? You want a long, deep sleep. Have
it. Your head is heavy. Very heavy. Your shoulders are
heavy. Sleep.

The pencil stops. Alan's eyes remain shut and his head
has sunk on his chest.

Can you hear me?
ALAN: Mmm.
DYSART: You can speak normally. Say Yes, if you can.
ALAN: Yes.
DYSART: Good boy. Now raise your head, and open your
eyes.

He does so.

Now, Alan, you're going to answer questions I'm going
to ask you. Do you understand?
ALAN: Yes.
DYSART: And when you wake up, you are going to re-
member everything you tell me. All right?
ALAN: Yes.
DYSART: Good. Now I want you to think back in time. You
are on that beach you told me about. The tide has
gone out, and you're making sandcastles. Above you,
staring down at you, is that great horse's head, and the
cream dropping from it. Can you see that?
ALAN: Yes.
DYSART: You ask him a question. 'Does the chin hurt?'
ALAN: Yes.
DYSART: Do you ask him aloud?
ALAN: No.
DYSART: And what does the horse say back?
ALAN: 'Yes.'
DYSART: Then what do you say?
ALAN: 'I'll take it out for you.'
DYSART: And he says?

ALAN: 'It never comes out. They have me in chains.'

DYSART: Like Jesus?

ALAN: Yes!

DYSART: Only his name isn't Jesus, is it?

ALAN: No.

DYSART: What is it?

ALAN: No one knows but him and me.

DYSART: You can tell me, Alan. Name him.

ALAN: Equus.

DYSART: Thank you. Does he live in all horses or just some?

ALAN: All.

DYSART: Good boy. Now: you leave the beach. You're in your bedroom at home. You're twelve years old. You're in front of the picture. You're looking at Equus from the foot of your bed. Would you like to kneel down?

ALAN: Yes.

DYSART: [*encouragingly*] Go on, then.

Alan kneels.

Now tell me. Why is Equus in chains?

ALAN: For the sins of the world.

DYSART: What does he say to you?

ALAN: 'I see you.' 'I will save you.'

DYSART: How?

ALAN: 'Bear you away. Two shall be one.'

DYSART: Horse and rider shall be one beast?

ALAN: One person!

DYSART: Go on.

ALAN: 'And my chinkle-chankle shall be in thy hand.'

DYSART: Chinkle-chankle? That's his mouth chain?

ALAN: Yes.

DYSART: Good. You can get up . . . Come on.

Alan rises.

Now: think of the stable. What is the stable? His Temple? His Holy of Holies?

ALAN: Yes.

DYSART: Where you wash him? Where you tend him, and brush him with many brushes?

76

ALAN: Yes.

DYSART: And there he spoke to you, didn't he? He looked at you with his gentle eyes, and spake unto you?

ALAN: Yes.

DYSART: What did he say? 'Ride me? Mount me, and ride me forth at night?'

ALAN: Yes.

DYSART: And you obeyed?

ALAN: Yes.

DYSART: How did you learn? By watching others?

ALAN: Yes.

DYSART: It must have been difficult. You bounced about?

ALAN: Yes.

DYSART: But he showed you, didn't he? Equus showed you the way.

ALAN: No!

DYSART: He didn't?

ALAN: He showed me nothing! He's a mean bugger! Ride —or fall! That's Straw Law.

DYSART: Straw Law?

ALAN: He was born in the straw, and this is his law.

DYSART: But you managed? You mastered him?

ALAN: Had to!

DYSART: And then you rode in secret?

ALAN: Yes.

DYSART: How often?

ALAN: Every three weeks. More, people would notice.

DYSART: On a particular horse?

ALAN: No.

DYSART: How did you get into the stable?

ALAN: Stole a key. Had it copied at Bryson's.

DYSART: Clever boy.

Alan smiles.

   Then you'd slip out of the house?

ALAN: Midnight! On the stroke!

DYSART: How far's the stable?

ALAN: Two miles.

Pause.

77

DYSART: Let's do it! Let's go riding! . . . Now!

He stands up, and pushes in his bench.

You are there now, in front of the stable door.

Alan turns upstage.

That key's in your hand. Go and open it.

20

Alan moves upstage, and mimes opening the door.
Soft light on the circle.
Humming from the Chorus: the Equus noise.
The horse actors enter, raise high their masks, and put
them on all together. They stand around the circle—
Nugget in the mouth of the tunnel.

DYSART: Quietly as possible. Dalton may still be awake.
Sssh . . . Quietly . . . Good. Now go in.

Alan steps secretly out of the square through the central
opening on to the circle, now glowing with a warm light.
He looks about him. The horses stamp uneasily: their
masks turn towards him.

You are on the inside now. All the horses are staring
at you. Can you see them?
ALAN: [*excited*] Yes!
DYSART: Which one are you going to take?
ALAN: Nugget.

Alan reaches up and mimes leading Nugget carefully
round the circle downstage with a rope, past all the horses
on the right.

DYSART: What colour is Nugget?

ALAN: Chestnut.

The horse picks his way with care. Alan halts him at the corner of the square.

DYSART: What do you do, first thing?
ALAN: Put on his sandals.
DYSART: Sandals?

He kneels, downstage centre.

ALAN: Sandals of majesty! . . . Made of sack.

He picks up the invisible sandals, and kisses them devoutly.

Tie them round his hooves.

He taps Nugget's right leg: the horse raises it and the boy mimes tying the sack round it.

DYSART: All four hooves?
ALAN: Yes.
DYSART: Then?
ALAN: Chinkle-chankle.

He mimes picking up the bridle and bit.

He doesn't like it so late, but he takes it for my sake. He bends for me. He stretches forth his neck to it.

Nugget bends his head down. Alan first ritually puts the bit into his own mouth, then crosses, and transfers it into Nugget's. He reaches up and buckles on the bridle. Then he leads him by the invisible reins, across the front of the stage and up round the left side of the circle. Nugget follows obediently.

ALAN: Buckle and lead out.
DYSART: No saddle?
ALAN: Never.

79

DYSART: Go on.

ALAN: Walk down the path behind. He's quiet. Always is, this bit. Meek and mild legs. At least till the field. Then there's trouble.

The horse jerks back. The mask tosses.

DYSART: What kind?

ALAN: Won't go in.

DYSART: Why not?

ALAN: It's his place of Ha Ha.

DYSART: What?

ALAN: Ha Ha.

DYSART: Make him go into it.

ALAN: [*whispering fiercely*] Come on! . . . Come on! . . .

He drags the horse into the square as Dysart steps out of it.

21

Nugget comes to a halt staring diagonally down what is now the field. The Equus noise dies away. The boy looks about him.

DYSART: [*from the circle*] Is it a big field?

ALAN: Huge!

DYSART: What's it like?

ALAN: Full of mist. Nettles on your feet.

He mimes taking off his shoes—and the sting.

   Ah!

DYSART: [*going back to his bench*] You take your shoes off?

ALAN: Everything.

DYSART: All your clothes?

ALAN: Yes.

He mimes undressing completely in front of the horse. When he is finished, and obviously quite naked, he throws out his arms and shows himself fully to his God, bowing his head before Nugget.

DYSART: Where do you leave them?
ALAN: Tree hole near the gate. No one could find them.

He walks upstage and crouches by the bench, stuffing the invisible clothes beneath it. Dysart sits again on the left bench, downstage beyond the circle.

DYSART: How does it feel now?
ALAN: [*holds himself*] Burns.
DYSART: Burns?
ALAN: The mist!
DYSART: Go on. Now what?
ALAN: The Manbit.

He reaches again under the bench and draws out an invisible stick.

DYSART: Manbit?
ALAN: The stick for my mouth.
DYSART: Your mouth?
ALAN: To bite on.
DYSART: Why? What for?
ALAN: So's it won't happen too quick.
DYSART: Is it always the same stick?
ALAN: Course. Sacred stick. Keep it in the hole. The Ark of the Manbit.
DYSART: And now what? . . . What do you do now?

Pause. He rises and approaches Nugget.

ALAN: Touch him!
DYSART: Where?
ALAN: [*in wonder*] All over. Everywhere. Belly. Ribs. His ribs are of ivory. Of great value! . . . His flank is cool. His nostrils open for me. His eyes shine. They can see in the dark . . . *Eyes!*—

81

Suddenly he dashes in distress to the farthest corner of the square.

DYSART: *Go on!* . . . Then?

Pause.

ALAN: Give sugar.
DYSART: A lump of sugar?

Alan returns to Nugget.

ALAN: His Last Supper.
DYSART: Last before what?
ALAN: Ha Ha.

He kneels before the horse, palms upward and joined together.

DYSART: Do you say anything when you give it to him?
ALAN: [*offering it*] Take my sins. Eat them for my sake . . .
   He always does.

Nugget bows the mask into Alan's palm, then takes a step back to eat.

   And then he's ready.
DYSART: You can get up on him now?
ALAN: Yes!
DYSART: Do it, then. Mount him.

Alan, lying before Nugget, stretches out on the square. He grasps the top of the thin metal pole embedded in the wood. He whispers his God's name ceremonially.

ALAN: Equus! . . . Equus! . . . Equus!

He pulls the pole upright. The actor playing Nugget leans forward and grabs it. At the same instant all the other horses lean forward around the circle, each placing a gloved hand on the rail. Alan rises and walks right back to the upstage corner, left.

Take me!

He runs and jumps high on to Nugget's back.

[*crying out*] Ah!
DYSART: What is it?
ALAN: Hurts!
DYSART: Hurts?
ALAN: Knives in his skin! Little knives—all inside my legs.

Nugget mimes restiveness.

ALAN: Stay, Equus. No one said Go! . . . That's it. He's good. Equus the Godslave, Faithful and True. Into my hands he commends himself—naked in his chinkle-chankle. [*he punches*] Stop it! . . . He wants to go so badly.
DYSART: Go, then. Leave me behind. Ride away now, Alan. Now! . . . Now you are alone with Equus.

Alan stiffens his body.

ALAN: [*ritually*] Equus—son of Fleckwus—son of Neckwus—Walk.

A hum from the Chorus.
Very slowly the horses standing on the circle begin to turn the square by gently pushing the wooden rail. Alan and his mount start to revolve. The effect, immediately, is of a statue being slowly turned round on a plinth. During the ride however the speed increases, and the light decreases until it is only a fierce spotlight on horse and rider, with the overspill glinting on the other masks leaning in towards them.

Here we go. The King rides out on Equus, mightiest of horses. Only I can ride him. He lets me turn him this way and that. His neck comes out of my body. It lifts

83

in the dark. Equus, my Godslave! . . . Now the King commands you. Tonight, we ride against them all.

DYSART: Who's all?

ALAN: My foes and His.

DYSART: Who are your foes?

ALAN: The Hosts of Hoover. The Hosts of Philco. The Hosts of Pifco. The House of Remington and all its tribe!

DYSART: Who are His foes?

ALAN: The Hosts of Jodhpur. The Hosts of Bowler and Gymkhana. All those who show him off for their vanity. Tie rosettes on his head for their vanity! Come on, Equus. Let's get them! . . . *Trot!*

The speed of the turning square increases.

Stead-y! Stead-y! Stead-y! Stead-y! Cowboys are watching! Take off their stetsons. They know who we are. They're admiring us! Bowing low unto us! Come on now—show them! *Canter!* . . . CANTER!

He whips Nugget.

And Equus the Mighty rose against All!
His enemies scatter, his enemies fall!
TURN!
Trample them, trample them,
Trample them, trample them,
TURN!
TURN! !
TURN! ! !

The Equus noise increases in volume.

[*shouting*] WEE! . . . WAA! . . . WONDERFUL! . . .
I'm stiff! Stiff in the wind!
My mane, stiff in the wind!
My flanks! *My* hooves!
Mane on my legs, on my flanks, like whips!
Raw!
Raw!

I'm raw! Raw!
Feel me on you! On you! On you! On you!
I want to be in you!
I want to BE you forever and ever!—
Equus, I love you!
Now!—
Bear me away!
Make us One Person!

He rides Equus frantically.

One Person! One Person! One Person! One Person!

He rises up on the horse's back, and calls like a trumpet.

Ha-HA! . . . Ha-HA! . . . Ha HA!

The trumpet turns to great cries.

HA-HA! HA-HA! HA-HA! HA-HA! HA! . . . HA! . . .
HAAAAA!

He twists like a flame.
Silence.
The turning square comes to a stop in the same position it
occupied at the opening of the Act.
Slowly the boy drops off the horse's back on to the ground.
He lowers his head and kisses Nugget's hoof.
Finally he flings back his head and cries up to him:

AMEN!

Nugget snorts, once.

BLACKOUT

ACT TWO

22

Darkness.
Lights come slowly up on Alan kneeling in the night at the hooves of Nugget. Slowly he gets up, climbing lovingly up the body of the horse until he can stand and kiss it. Dysart sits on the downstage bench where he began Act One.

DYSART: With one particular horse, called Nugget, he embraces. He showed me how he stands with it afterwards in the night, one hand on its chest, one on its neck, like a frozen tango dancer, inhaling its cold sweet breath. 'Have you noticed,' he said, 'about horses: how they'll stand one hoof on its end, like those girls in the ballet?'

Alan leads Nugget out of the square. Dysart rises. The horse walks away up the tunnel and disappears. The boy comes downstage and sits on the bench Dysart has vacated. Dysart crosses downstage and moves slowly up round the circle, until he reaches the central entrance to the square.

Now he's gone off to rest, leaving me alone with Equus. I can hear the creature's voice. It's calling me out of the black cave of the Psyche. I shove in my dim little torch, and there he stands—waiting for me. He raises his matted head. He opens his great square teeth, and says —[*mocking*] 'Why? . . . Why Me? . . . Why—ultimately —Me? . . . Do you really imagine you can account for

Me? Totally, infallibly, inevitably account for Me? . . .
Poor Doctor Dysart!'

He enters the square.

Of course I've stared at such images before. Or been
stared at by them, whichever way you look at it. And
weirdly often now with me the feeling is that *they* are
staring at *us*—that in some quite palpable way they pre-
cede us. Meaningless, but unsettling . . . In either case,
this one is the most alarming yet. It asks questions I've
avoided all my professional life. [*Pause*] A child is
born into a world of phenomena all equal in their power
to enslave. It sniffs—it sucks—it strokes it eyes over
the whole uncomfortable range. Suddenly one strikes.
Why? Moments snap together like magnets, forging a
chain of shackles. Why? I can trace them. I can even,
with time, pull them apart again. But why at the start
they were ever magnetized at all—just those particular
moments of experience and no others—I don't know.
And nor does anyone else. Yet *if* I don't know—if I can
never know that—then what am I doing here? I don't
mean clinically doing or socially doing—I mean *funda-
mentally!* These questions, these Whys, are fundamental
—yet they have no place in a consulting room. So then,
do I? . . . This is the feeling more and more with me—
No Place. Displacement. . . . 'Account for me,' says
staring Equus. 'First account for Me! . . .' I fancy this
is more than menopause.

Nurse rushes in.

NURSE: Doctor! . . . Doctor! There's a terrible scene with
the Strang boy. His mother came to visit him, and I
gave her the tray to take in. He threw it at her. She's
saying the most dreadful things.

*Alan springs up, down left. Dora springs up, down right.
They face each other across the bottom end of the stage.
It is observable that at the start of this Act Frank is not
sitting beside his wife on their bench. It is hopefully not*

observable that he is placed among the audience upstage, in the gloom, by the central tunnel.

DORA: Don't you dare! *Don't you dare!*
DYSART: Is she still there?
NURSE: Yes!

He quickly leaves the square, followed by the Nurse. Dora moves towards her son.

DORA: Don't you look at me like that! I'm not a doctor, you know, who'll take anything. Don't you dare give me that stare, young man!

She slaps his face. Dysart joins them.

DYSART: Mrs Strang!
DORA: I know your stares. They don't work on me!
DYSART: [*to her*] Leave this room.
DORA: What did you say?
DYSART: I tell you to leave here at once.

Dora hesitates. Then:

DORA: Goodbye, Alan.

She walks past her son, and round into the square. Dysart follows her. Both are very upset. Alan returns to his bench and Nurse to her place.

23

Lights up on the square.

DYSART: I must ask you never to come here again.
DORA: Do you think I want to? Do you think I want to?
DYSART: Mrs Strang, what on earth has got into you? Can't you see the boy is highly distressed?

DORA: [ironic] Really?

DYSART: Of course! He's at a most delicate stage of treatment. He's totally exposed. Ashamed. Everything you can imagine!

DORA: [exploding] And me? What about me? . . . What do you think I am? . . . I'm a parent, of course—so it doesn't count. That's a dirty word in here, isn't it, 'parent'?

DYSART: You know that's not true.

DORA: Oh, I know. I know, all right! I've heard it all my life. It's *our* fault. Whatever happens, *we* did it. Alan's just a little victim. He's really done nothing at all! [savagely] What do you have to do in this world to get any sympathy—blind animals?

DYSART: Sit down, Mrs Strang.

DORA: [ignoring him: more and more urgently] Look, Doctor: you don't have to live with this. Alan is one patient to you: one out of many. He's my son. I lie awake every night thinking about it. Frank lies there beside me. I can hear him. Neither of us sleeps all night. You come to us and say Who forbids television? who does what behind whose back?—as if we're criminals. Let me tell you something. We're not criminals. We've done nothing wrong. We loved Alan. We gave him the best love we could. All right, we quarrel sometimes—all parents quarrel—we always make it up. My husband is a good man. He's an upright man, religion or no religion. He cares for his home, for the world, and for his boy. Alan had love and care and treats, and as much fun as any boy in the world. I know about loveless homes: I was a teacher. Our home wasn't loveless. I know about privacy too—not invading a child's privacy. All right, Frank may be at fault there—he digs into him too much—but nothing in excess. He's not a bully . . . [gravely] No, doctor. Whatever's happened has happened *because of Alan*. Alan is himself. Every soul is itself. If you added up everything we ever did to him, from his first day on earth to this, you wouldn't find why he did this terrible thing—because that's *him*: not just all of our things added up. Do you understand what I'm saying? I want you to understand, because I

90

lie awake and awake thinking it out, and I want you to know that I deny it absolutely what he's doing now, staring at me, attacking me for what *he's* done, for what *he* is! [*pause: calmer*] You've got your words, and I've got mine. You call it a complex, I suppose. But if you knew God, Doctor, you would know about the Devil. You'd know the Devil isn't made by what mummy says and daddy says. The Devil's *there*. It's an old-fashioned word, but a true thing . . . I'll go. What I did in there was inexcusable. I only know he was my little Alan, and then the Devil came.

She leaves the square, and resumes her place. Dysart watches her go, then leaves himself by the opposite entrance, and approaches Alan.

24

Seated on his bench, the boy glares at him.

DYSART: I thought you liked your mother.

Silence.

She doesn't know anything, you know. I haven't told her what you told me. You do know that, don't you?
ALAN: It was lies anyway.
DYSART: What?
ALAN: You and your pencil. Just a con trick, that's all.
DYSART: What do you mean?
ALAN: Made me say a lot of lies.
DYSART: Did it? . . . Like what?
ALAN: All of it. Everything I said. Lot of lies.

Pause.

DYSART: I see.
ALAN: You ought to be locked up. Your bloody tricks.

DYSART: I thought you liked tricks.

ALAN: It'll be the drug next. I know.

Dysart turns, sharply.

DYSART: What drug?

ALAN: I've heard. I'm not ignorant. I know what you get up to in here. Shove needles in people, pump them full of truth drug, so they can't help saying things. That's next, isn't it?

Pause.

DYSART: Alan, do you know why you're here?

ALAN: So you can give me truth drugs.

He glares at him.
Dysart leaves abruptly, and returns to the square.

25

Hesther comes in simultaneously from the other side.

DYSART: [*agitated*] He actually thinks they exist! And of course he wants one.

HESTHER: It doesn't sound like that to me.

DYSART: Of course he does. Why mention them otherwise? He wants a way to speak. To finally tell me what happened in that stable. Tape's too isolated, and hypnosis is a trick. At least that's the pretence.

HESTHER: Does he still say that today?

DYSART: I haven't seen him. I cancelled his appointment this morning, and let him stew in his own anxiety. Now I am almost tempted to play a real trick on him.

HESTHER: [*sitting*] Like what?

DYSART: The old placebo.

HESTHER: You mean a harmless pill?

DYSART: Full of *alleged* Truth Drug. Probably an aspirin.

HESTHER: But he'd deny it afterwards. Same thing all over.

DYSART: No. Because he's ready to abreact.

HESTHER: Abreact?

DYSART: Live it all again. He won't be able to deny it after that, because he'll have shown me. Not just told me—but acted it out in front of me.

HESTHER: Can you get him to do that?

DYSART: I think so. He's nearly done it already. Under all that glowering, he trusts me. Do you realise that?

HESTHER: [warmly] I'm sure he does.

DYSART: Poor bloody fool.

HESTHER: Don't start that again.

Pause.

DYSART: [quietly] Can you think of anything worse one can do to anybody than take away their worship?

HESTHER: Worship?

DYSART: Yes, that word again!

HESTHER: Aren't you being a little extreme?

DYSART: Extremity's the point.

HESTHER: Worship isn't destructive, Martin. I know that.

DYSART: I don't. I only know it's the core of his life. What else has he got? Think about him. He can hardly read. He knows no physics or engineering to make the world real for him. No paintings to show him how others have enjoyed it. No music except television jingles. No history except tales from a desperate mother. No friends. Not one kid to give him a joke, or make him know himself more moderately. He's a modern citizen for whom society doesn't exist. He lives *one hour* every three weeks —howling in a mist. And after the service kneels to a slave who stands over him obviously and unthrowably his master. With my body I thee worship! . . . Many men have less vital with their wives.

Pause.

HESTHER: All the same, they don't usually blind their wives, do they?

DYSART: Oh, come on!

HESTHER: Well, do they?

DYSART: [*sarcastically*] You mean he's dangerous? A violent, dangerous madman who's going to run round the country doing it again and again?

HESTHER: I mean he's in pain, Martin. He's been in pain for most of his life. That much, at least, you *know*.

DYSART: Possibly.

HESTHER: *Possibly? !* . . . That cut-off little figure you just described must have been in pain for years.

DYSART: [*doggedly*] Possibly.

HESTHER: And you can take it away.

DYSART: Still—possibly.

HESTHER: Then that's enough. That simply has to be enough for you, surely?

DYSART: No!

HESTHER: Why not?

DYSART: Because it's his.

HESTHER: I don't understand.

DYSART: His pain. His own. He made it.

Pause.

[*earnestly*] Look . . . to go through life and call it yours —*your life*—you first have to get your own pain. Pain that's unique to you. You can't just dip into the common bin and say 'That's enough!' . . . He's done that. All right, he's sick. He's full of misery and fear. He was dangerous, and could be again, though I doubt it. But that boy has known a passion more ferocious than I have felt in any second of my life. And let me tell you something: I envy it.

HESTHER: You can't.

DYSART: [*vehemently*] Don't you see? That's the Accusation! That's what his stare has been saying to me all the time. '*At least I galloped! When did you?*' . . . [*simply*] I'm jealous, Hester. Jealous of Alan Strang.

HESTHER: That's absurd.

DYSART: Is it? . . . I go on about my wife. That smug woman by the fire. Have you thought of the fellow on the other side of it? The finicky, critical husband looking through his art books on mythical Greece. What

94

worship has *he* ever known? Real worship! Without worship you shrink, it's as brutal as that . . . I shrank my *own* life. No one can do it for you. I settled for being pallid and provincial, out of my own eternal timidity. The old story of bluster, and do bugger-all . . . I imply that we can't have children: but actually, it's only me. I had myself tested behind her back. The lowest sperm count you could find. And I never told her. That's all I need—her sympathy mixed with resentment . . . I tell everyone Margaret's the puritan, I'm the pagan. Some pagan! Such wild returns I make to the womb of civilization. Three weeks a year in the Peleponnese, every bed booked in advance, every meal paid for by vouchers, cautious jaunts in hired Fiats, suitcase crammed with Kao-Pectate! Such a fantastic surrender to the primitive. And I use that word endlessly: 'primitive'. 'Oh, the primitive world,' I say. 'What instinctual truths were lost with it!' And while I sit there, baiting a poor unimaginative woman with the word, that freaky boy tries to conjure the reality! I sit looking at pages of centaurs trampling the soil of Argos—and outside my window he is trying to *become one,* in a Hampshire field! . . . I watch that woman knitting, night after night—a woman I haven't *kissed* in six years—and he stands in the dark for an hour, sucking the sweat off his God's hairy cheek! [*pause*] Then in the morning, I put away my books on the cultural shelf, close up the koda-chrome snaps of Mount Olympus, touch my reproduction statue of Dionysus for luck—and go off to hospital to treat him for insanity. Do you see?

HESTHER: The boy's in pain, Martin. That's all I see. In the end . . . I'm sorry.

He looks at her. Alan gets up from his bench and stealthily places an envelope in the left-hand entrance of the square, then goes back and sits with his back to the audience, as if watching television.
Hesther rises.

HESTHER: That stare of his. Have you thought it might not be accusing you at all?

95

DYSART: What then?

HESTHER: Claiming you.

DYSART: For what?

HESTHER: [*mischievously*] A new God.

Pause.

DYSART: Too conventional, for him. Finding a religion in Psychiatry is really for very ordinary patients.

She laughs.

HESTHER: Maybe he just wants a new Dad. Or is that too conventional too? . . . Since you're questioning your profession anyway, perhaps you ought to try it and see.

DYSART: [*amused*] I'll talk to you.

HESTHER: Goodbye.

She smiles, and leaves him.

26

Dysart becomes aware of the letter lying on the floor. He picks it up, opens and reads it.

ALAN: [*speaking stiffly, as Dysart reads*] 'It is all true, what I said after you tapped the pencil. I'm sorry if I said different. Post Scriptum: I know why I'm in here.'

Pause.

DYSART: [*calling, joyfully*] Nurse!

Nurse comes in.

NURSE: Yes, Doctor?

DYSART: [*trying to conceal his pleasure*] Good evening!

NURSE: You're in late tonight.

DYSART: Yes! . . . Tell me, is the Strang boy in bed yet?

NURSE: Oh, no, Doctor. He's bound to be upstairs looking at television. He always watches to the last possible moment. He doesn't like going to his room at all.

DYSART: You mean he's still having nightmares?

NURSE: He had a bad one last night.

DYSART: Would you ask him to come down here, please?

NURSE: [faint surprise] Now?

DYSART: I'd like a word with him.

NURSE: [puzzled] Very good, Doctor.

DYSART: If he's not back in his room by lights out, tell Night Nurse not to worry. I'll see he gets back to bed all right. And would you phone my home and tell my wife I may be in late?

NURSE: Yes, Doctor.

DYSART: Ask him to come straight away, please.

Nurse goes to the bench, taps Alan on the shoulder, whispers her message in his ear, and returns to her place. Alan stands up and pauses for a second—then steps into the square.

27

He stands in the doorway, depressed.

DYSART: Hallo.

ALAN: Hallo.

DYSART: I got your letter. Thank you. [pause] Also the Post Scriptum.

ALAN: [defensively] That's the right word. My mum told me. It's Latin for 'After-writing'.

DYSART: How are you feeling?

ALAN: All right.

DYSART: I'm sorry I didn't see you today.

ALAN: You were fed up with me.

DYSART: Yes. [pause] Can I make it up to you now?

ALAN: What'd you mean?
DYSART: I thought we'd have a session.
ALAN: [startled] Now?
DYSART: Yes! At dead of night! . . . Better than going to sleep, isn't it?

The boy flinches.

Alan—look. Everything I say has a trick or a catch. Everything I do is a trick or a catch. That's all I know to do. But they work—and you know that. Trust me.

Pause.

ALAN: You got another trick, then?
DYSART: Yes.
ALAN: A truth drug?
DYSART: If you like.
ALAN: What's it do?
DYSART: Make it easier for you to talk.
ALAN: Like you can't help yourself?
DYSART: That's right. Like you have to speak the truth at all costs. And all of it.

Pause.

ALAN: [slyly] Comes in a needle, doesn't it?
DYSART: No.
ALAN: Where is it?
DYSART: [indicating his pocket] In here.
ALAN: Let's see.

Dysart solemnly takes a bottle of pills out of his pocket.

DYSART: There.
ALAN: [suspicious] That really it?
DYSART: It is . . . Do you want to try it?
ALAN: No.
DYSART: I think you do.
ALAN: I don't. Not at all.
DYSART: Afterwards you'd sleep. You'd have no bad

dreams all night. Probably many nights, from then
on . . .

Pause.

ALAN: How long's it take to work?
DYSART: It's instant. Like coffee.
ALAN: [*half believing*] It isn't!
DYSART: I promise you . . . Well?
ALAN: Can I have a fag?
DYSART: Pill first. Do you want some water?
ALAN: No.

*Dysart shakes one out on to his palm. Alan hesitates for a
second—then takes it and swallows it.*

DYSART: Then you can chase it down with this. Sit down.

He offers him a cigarette, and lights it for him.

ALAN: [*nervous*] What happens now?
DYSART: We wait for it to work.
ALAN: What'll I feel first?
DYSART: Nothing much. After a minute, about a hundred
   green snakes should come out of that cupboard singing
   the Hallelujah Chorus.
ALAN: [*annoyed*] *I'm serious!*
DYSART: [*earnestly*] You'll feel nothing. Nothing's going to
   happen now but what you want to happen. You're
   not going to say anything to me but what you want to
   say. Just relax. Lie back and finish your fag.

*Alan stares at him. Then accepts the situation, and lies
back.*

DYSART: Good boy.
ALAN: I bet this room's heard some funny things.
DYSART: It certainly has.
ALAN: I like it.
DYSART: This room?
ALAN: Don't you?

99

DYSART: Well, there's not much to like, is there?

ALAN: How long am I going to be in here?

DYSART: It's hard to say. I quite see you want to leave.

ALAN: No.

DYSART: You don't?

ALAN: Where would I go?

DYSART: Home. . . .

The boy looks at him. Dysart crosses and sits on the rail upstage, his feet on the bench. A pause.

Actually, I'd like to leave this room and never see it again in my life.

ALAN: [*surprise*] Why?

DYSART: I've been in it too long.

ALAN: Where would you go?

DYSART: Somewhere.

ALAN: Secret?

DYSART: Yes. There's a sea—a great sea—I love . . . It's where the Gods used to go to bathe.

ALAN: What Gods?

DYSART: The old ones. Before they died.

ALAN: Gods don't die.

DYSART: Yes, they do.

Pause.

There's a village I spent one night in, where I'd like to live. It's all white.

ALAN: How would you Nosey Parker, though? You wouldn't have a room for it any more.

DYSART: I wouldn't mind. I don't actually enjoy being a Nosey Parker, you know.

ALAN: Then why do it?

DYSART: Because you're unhappy.

ALAN: So are you.

Dysart looks at him sharply. Alan sits up in alarm.

Oooh, I didn't mean that!

DYSART: Didn't you?

100

ALAN: Here—is that how it works? Things just slip out, not feeling anything?

DYSART: That's right.

ALAN: But it's so quick!

DYSART: I told you: it's instant.

ALAN: [*delighted*] It's wicked, isn't it? I mean, you can say anything under it.

DYSART: Yes.

ALAN: Ask me a question.

DYSART: Tell me about Jill.

Pause. The boy turns away.

ALAN: There's nothing to tell.

DYSART: Nothing?

ALAN: No.

DYSART: Well, for example—is she pretty? You've never described her.

ALAN: She's all right.

DYSART: What colour hair?

ALAN: Dunno.

DYSART: Is it long or short?

ALAN: Dunno.

DYSART: [*lightly*] You must know that.

ALAN: I don't remember. *I don't!*

Dysart rises and comes down to him. He takes the cigarette out of his hand.

DYSART: [*firmly*] Lie back . . . Now listen. You have to do this. And now. You are going to tell me everything that happened with this girl. And not just *tell* me—*show* me. Act it out, if you like—even more than you did when I tapped the pencil. I want you to feel free to do absolutely anything in this room. The pill will help you. I will help you . . . Now, where does she live?

A long pause.

ALAN: [*tight*] Near the stables. About a mile.

101

Dysart steps down out of the square as Jill enters it. He sits again on the downstage bench.

28

The light grows warmer.

JILL: It's called The China Pantry.

She comes down and sits casually on the rail. Her manner is open and lightly provocative. During these scenes Alan acts directly with her, and never looks over at Dysart when he replies to him.

When Daddy disappeared, she was left without a bean. She had to earn her own living. I must say she did jolly well, considering she was never trained in business.
DYSART: What do you mean, 'disappeared'?
ALAN: [*to Dysart*] He ran off. No one ever saw him again.
JILL: Just left a note on her dressing table saying 'Sorry. I've had it.' Just like that. She never got over it. It turned her right off men. All my dates have to be sort of secret. I mean, she knows about them, but I can't ever bring anyone back home. She's so rude to them.
ALAN: [*to Dysart*] She was always looking.
DYSART: At you?
ALAN: [*to Dysart*] Saying stupid things.

She jumps off the bench.

JILL: You've got super eyes.
ALAN: [*to Dysart*] Anyway, *she* was the one who had them.

She sits next to him. Embarrassed, the boy tries to move away as far as he can.

JILL: There was an article in the paper last week saying what points about boys fascinate girls. They said Num-

ber One is bottoms. I think it's eyes every time . . .
They fascinate you too, don't they?

ALAN: Me?

JILL: [sly] Or is it only horses' eyes?

ALAN: [startled] What'd you mean?

JILL: I saw you staring into Nugget's eyes yesterday for
ages. I spied on you through the door!

ALAN: [hotly] There must have been something in it!

JILL: You're a real Man of Mystery, aren't you?

ALAN: [to Dysart] Sometimes, it was like she knew.

DYSART: Did you ever hint?

ALAN: [to Dysart] Course not!

JILL: I love horses' eyes. The way you can see yourself in
them. D'you find them sexy?

ALAN: [outraged] What? !

JILL: Horses.

ALAN: Don't be daft!

He springs up, and away from her.

JILL: Girls do. I mean, they go through a period when
they pat them and kiss them a lot. I know I did. I suppose it's just a substitute, really.

ALAN: [to Dysart] That kind of thing, all the time. Until
one night . . .

DYSART: Yes? What?

ALAN: [to Dysart: defensively] She did it! Not me. It was
her idea, the whole thing! . . . She got me into it!

DYSART: What are you saying? 'One night': go on from
there.

A pause.

ALAN: [to Dysart] Saturday night. We were just closing up.

JILL: How would you like to take me out?

ALAN: What?

JILL: [coolly] How would you like to take me out tonight?

ALAN: I've got to go home.

JILL: What for?

He tries to escape upstage.

ALAN: They expect me.

JILL: Ring up and say you're going out.

ALAN: I can't.

JILL: Why?

ALAN: They expect me.

JILL: Look. Either we go out together and have some fun, or you go back to your boring home, *as usual,* and I go back to mine. That's the situation, isn't it?

ALAN: Well . . . where would we go?

JILL: The pictures! There's a skinflick over in Winchester! I've never seen one, have you?

ALAN: No.

JILL: Wouldn't you like to? *I* would. All those heavy Swedes, panting at each other! . . . What d'you say?

ALAN: [*grinning*] Yeh! . . .

JILL: Good! . . .

He turns away.

DYSART: Go on, please.

He steps off the square.

ALAN: [*to Dysart*] I'm tired now!

DYSART: Come on now. You can't stop there.

He storms round the circle to Dysart, and faces him directly.

ALAN: I'm *tired!* I want to go to bed!

DYSART: [*sharply*] Well, you can't. I want to hear about the film.

ALAN: [*hostile*] Hear what? . . . *What?* . . . It was bloody awful!

The actors playing horses come swiftly on to the square, dressed in sports coats or raincoats. They move the benches to be parallel with the audience, and sit on them—staring out front.

DYSART: Why?

ALAN: Nosey Parker!

DYSART: *Why?*

ALAN: *Because!* . . . Well—we went into the Cinema!

29

A burst of Rock music, instantly fading down. Lights darken.

Alan re-enters the square. Jill rises and together they grope their way to the downstage bench, as if in a dark auditorium.

ALAN: [*To Dysart*] The whole place was full of men. Jill was the only girl.

They push by a patron seated at the end, and sit side by side, staring up at the invisible screen, located above the heads of the main audience. A spotlight hits the boy's face.

We sat down and the film came on. It was daft. Nothing happened for ages. There was this girl Brita, who was sixteen. She went to stay in this house, where there was an older boy. He kept giving her looks, but she ignored him completely. In the end she took a shower. She went into the bathroom and took off all her clothes. The lot. Very slowly. . . . What she didn't know was the boy was looking through the door all the time. . . . [*he starts to become excited*] It was fantastic! The water fell on her breasts, bouncing down her. . . .

Frank steps into the square furtively from the back, hat in hand, and stands looking about for a place.

DYSART: Was that the first time you'd seen a girl naked?

ALAN: [*to Dysart*] Yes! You couldn't see everything, though . . . . [*looking about him*] All round me they were all looking. All the men—staring up like they were in

105

church. Like they were a sort of congregation. And then—[*he sees his father*] *Ah!*

At the same instant Frank sees him.

FRANK: Alan!
ALAN: God!
JILL: What is it?
ALAN: *Dad!*
JILL: *Where?*
ALAN: At the back! *He saw me!*
JILL: You sure?
ALAN: Yes!
FRANK: [*calling*] Alan!
ALAN: Oh God!

He tries to hide his face in the girl's shoulder. His father comes down the aisle towards him.

FRANK: Alan! You can hear me! Don't pretend!
PATRONS: *Ssssh!*
FRANK: [*approaching the row of seats*] Do I have to come and fetch you out? . . . Do I? . . .

Cries of 'Sssh!' and 'Shut up!'

Do I, Alan?
ALAN: [*through gritted teeth*] Oh fuck!

He gets up as the noise increases. Jill gets up too and follows him.

DYSART: You went?
ALAN: [*to Dysart*] What else could I do? He kept shouting. Everyone was saying Shut up!

They go out, right, through the group of Patrons—who rise protesting as they pass, quickly replace the benches and leave the square.
Dysart enters it.

30

*Light brightens from the cinema, but remains cold: streets
at night.*
*The three walk round the circle downstage in a line:
Frank leading, wearing his hat. He halts in the middle of
the left rail, and stands staring straight ahead of him, rigid
with embarrassment.*
Alan is very agitated.

ALAN: [*to Dysart*] We went into the street, all three of us.
It was weird. We just stood there by the bus stop—like
we were three people in a queue, and we didn't know
each other. Dad was all white and sweaty. He didn't
look at us at all. It must have gone on for about five
minutes. I tried to speak. I said—[*to his father*] I—I—
I've never been there before. Honest . . . Never . . .
[*to Dysart*] He didn't seem to hear. Jill tried.

JILL: It's true, Mr Strang. It wasn't Alan's idea to go
there. It was mine.

ALAN: [*to Dysart*] He just went on staring, straight ahead.
It was awful.

JILL: I'm not shocked by films like that. I think they're
just silly.

ALAN: [*to Dysart*] The bus wouldn't come. We just stood
and stood. . . . Then suddenly he spoke.

Frank takes off his hat.

FRANK: [*stiffly*] I'd like you to know something. Both of
you. I came here tonight to see the Manager. He asked
me to call on him for business purposes. I happen to be
a printer, Miss. A picture house needs posters. That's
entirely why I'm here. To discuss posters. While I was
waiting I happened to glance in, that's all. I can only
say I'm going to complain to the council. I had no

idea they showed films like this. I'm certainly going to refuse my services.

JILL: [kindly] Yes, of course.

FRANK: So long as that's understood.

ALAN: [to Dysart] Then the bus came along.

FRANK: Come along now, Alan.

He moves away downstage.

ALAN: No.

FRANK: [turning] No fuss, please. Say Goodnight to the young lady.

ALAN: [timid but firm] No. I'm stopping here . . . I've got to see her home . . . It's proper.

Pause.

FRANK: [as dignified as possible] Very well. I'll see you when you choose to return. Very well then . . . Yes . . .

He walks back to his original seat, next to his wife. He stares across the square at his son—who stares back at him. Then, slowly, he sits.

ALAN: [to Dysart] And he got in, and we didn't. He sat down and looked at me through the glass. And I saw . . .

DYSART: [soft] What?

ALAN: [to Dysart] His face. It was scared.

DYSART: Of you?

ALAN: [to Dysart] It was terrible. We had to walk home. Four miles. I got the shakes.

DYSART: You were scared too?

ALAN: [to Dysart] It was like a hole had been drilled in my tummy. A hole—right here. And the air was getting in!

He starts to walk upstage, round the circle.

31

The girl stays still.

JILL: [*aware of other people looking*] Alan . . .

ALAN: [*to Dysart*] People kept turning round in the street to look.

JILL: Alan!

ALAN: [*to Dysart*] I kept seeing him, just as he drove off. Scared of me. . . . And me scared of *him*. . . . I kept thinking—all those airs he put on! . . . 'Receive my meaning. Improve your mind!' . . . All those nights he said he'd be in late. 'Keep my supper hot, Dora!' 'Your poor father: he works so hard!' . . . Bugger! Old bugger! . . . Filthy old bugger!

He stops, clenching his fists.

JILL: Hey! Wait for me!

She runs after him. He waits.

What are you thinking about?

ALAN: Nothing.

JILL: Mind my own beeswax?

She laughs.

ALAN: [*to Dysart*] And suddenly she began to laugh.

JILL: I'm sorry. But it's pretty funny, when you think of it.

ALAN: [*bewildered*] What?

JILL: Catching him like that! I mean, it's terrible—but it's very funny.

ALAN: Yeh!

He turns from her.

JILL: No, wait! . . . I'm sorry. I know you're upset. But it's
not the end of the world, is it? I mean, what was he
doing? Only what we were. Watching a silly film. It's a
case of like father like son, I'd say! . . . I mean, when
that girl was taking a shower, you were pretty interested,
weren't you?

He turns round and looks at her.

We keep saying old people are square. Then when they
suddenly aren't—we don't like it!
DYSART: What did you think about that?
ALAN: [*to Dysart*] I don't know. I kept looking at all the
people in the street. They were mostly men coming out
of pubs. I suddenly thought—*they all do it! All of
them!* . . . They're not just Dads—they're people with
pricks! . . . And Dad—he's just not Dad either. He's a
man with a prick too. You know, I'd never thought
about it.

Pause.

We went into the country.

*He walks again. Jill follows. They turn the corner and
come downstage, right.*

We kept walking. I just thought about Dad, and how he
was nothing special—just a poor old sod on his own.

He stops.

[*to Jill: realising it*] Poor old sod!
JILL: That's right!
ALAN: [*grappling with it*] I mean, what else has he got? . . .
He's got mum, of course, but well—she—she—she——
JILL: She doesn't give him anything?
ALAN: That's right. I bet you . . . She doesn't give him
anything. That's right . . . That's really right! . . . She
likes Ladies and Gentlemen. Do you understand what I
mean?

JILL: [*mischievously*] Ladies and gentlemen aren't naked?

ALAN: That's right! Never! . . . *Never!* That would be disgusting! She'd have to put bowler hats on them! . . . Jodhpurs!

Jill laughs.

DYSART: Was that the first time you ever thought anything like that about your mother? . . . I mean, that she was unfair to your dad?

ALAN: [*to Dysart*] Absolutely!

DYSART: How did you feel?

ALAN: [*to Dysart*] Sorry. I mean for him. Poor old sod, that's what I felt—he's just like me! He hates ladies and gents just like me! Posh things—and la-di-da. He goes off by himself at night, and does his own secret thing which no one'll know about, just like me! There's no difference—he's just the same as me—just the same!—

He stops in distress, then bolts back a little upstage.

Christ!

DYSART: [*sternly*] Go on.

ALAN: [*to Dysart*] I can't.

DYSART: Of course you can. You're doing wonderfully.

ALAN: [*to Dysart*] No, please. *Don't make me!*

DYSART: [*firm*] Don't think: just answer. You were happy at that second, weren't you? When you realised about your dad. How lots of people have secrets, not just you?

ALAN: [*to Dysart*] Yes.

DYSART: You felt sort of free, didn't you? I mean, free to do anything?

ALAN: [*to Dysart, looking at Jill*] Yes!

DYSART: What was she doing?

ALAN: [*to Dysart*] Holding my hand.

DYSART: And that was good?

ALAN: [*to Dysart*] Oh, yes!

DYSART: Remember what you thought. *As if it's happening to you now. This very moment* . . . What's in your head?

ALAN: [*to Dysart*] Her eyes. *She's* the one with eyes! . . . I

111

keep looking at them, because I really want—

DYSART: To look at her breasts?

ALAN: [to Dysart] Yes.

DYSART: Like in the film.

ALAN: [to Dysart] Yes . . . Then she starts to scratch my hand.

JILL: You're really very nice, you know that?

ALAN: [to Dysart] Moving her nails on the back. Her face so warm. Her eyes.

DYSART: You want her very much?

ALAN: [to Dysart] Yes . . .

JILL: I love your eyes.

She kisses him.

[whispering] Let's go!

ALAN: Where?

JILL: I know a place. It's right near here.

ALAN: Where?

JILL: Surprise! . . . Come on!

She darts away round the circle, across the stage and up the left side.

Come *on!*

ALAN: [to Dysart] She runs ahead. I follow. And then—and then—!

He halts.

DYSART: What?

ALAN: [to Dysart] I see what she means.

DYSART: What? . . . Where are you? . . . Where has she taken you?

ALAN: [to Jill] The Stables?

JILL: Of course!

32

Chorus makes a warning hum.
The horses actors enter, and ceremonially put on their
masks—first raising them high above their heads. Nugget
stands in the central tunnel.

ALAN: [*recoiling*] No!
JILL: Where else? They're perfect!
ALAN: No!

He turns his head from her.

JILL: Or do you want to go home now and face your dad?
ALAN: No!
JILL: Then come on!

He edges nervously past the horse standing at the left,
which turns its neck and even moves a challenging step
after him.

ALAN: Why not your place?
JILL: I can't. Mother doesn't like me bringing back boys.
  I told you. . . . Anyway, the Barn's better.
ALAN: No!
JILL: All that straw. It's cosy.
ALAN: No.
JILL: *Why not?*
ALAN: Them!
JILL: Dalton will be in bed . . . What's the matter? . . .
  Don't you want to?
ALAN: [*aching to*] Yes!
JILL: So?
ALAN: [*desperate*] Them! . . . Them! . . .
JILL: *Who?*
ALAN: [*low*] Horses.
JILL: *Horses?* . . . You're really dotty, aren't you? . . .

What do you mean?

He starts shaking.

Oh, you're freezing . . . Let's get under the straw. You'll be warm there.

ALAN: [*pulling away*] No!

JILL: What on earth's the matter with you? . . .

Silence. He won't look at her.

Look, if the sight of horses offends you, my lord, we can just shut the door. You won't have to see them. All right?

DYSART: What door is that? In the barn?

ALAN: [*to Dysart*] Yes.

DYSART: So what do you do? You go in?

ALAN: [*to Dysart*] Yes.

33

A rich light falls.

Furtively Alan enters the square from the top end, and Jill follows. The horses on the circle retire out of sight on either side. Nugget retreats up the tunnel and stands where he can just be glimpsed in the dimness.

DYSART: Into the Temple? The Holy of Holies?

ALAN: [*to Dysart: desperate*] What else can I do? . . . I can't say! I can't tell her . . . [*to Jill*] Shut it tight.

JILL: All right . . . You're crazy!

ALAN: Lock it.

JILL: Lock?

ALAN: Yes.

JILL: It's just an old door. What's the matter with you? They're in their boxes. They can't get out . . . Are you all right?

ALAN: Why?

JILL: You look weird.

ALAN: *Lock it!*

JILL: Ssssh! D'you want to wake up Dalton? . . . Stay there, idiot.

She mimes locking a heavy door, upstage.

DYSART: Describe the barn, please.

ALAN: [*walking round it: to Dysart*] Large room. Straw everywhere. Some tools . . . [*as if picking it up off the rail where he left it in Act One*] A hoof pick! . . .

He 'drops' it hastily, and dashes away from the spot.

DYSART: *Go on.*

ALAN: [*to Dysart*] At the end this big door. Behind it—

DYSART: Horses.

ALAN: [*to Dysart*] Yes.

DYSART: How many?

ALAN: [*to Dysart*] Six.

DYSART: Jill closes the door so you can't see them?

ALAN: [*to Dysart*] Yes.

DYSART: And then? . . . What happens now? . . . Come on, Alan. Show me.

JILL: See, it's all shut. There's just us . . . Let's sit down. Come on.

They sit together on the same bench, left.

Hallo.

ALAN: [*quickly*] Hallo.

She kisses him lightly. He responds. Suddenly a faint trampling of hooves, off-stage, makes him jump up.

JILL: What is it?

He turns his head upstage, listening.

Relax. There's no one there. Come here.

115

She touches his hand. He turns to her again.

　　You're very gentle. I love that . . .
ALAN: So are you . . . I mean . . .

He kisses her spontaneously. The hooves trample again, harder. He breaks away from her abruptly towards the upstage corner.

JILL: [*rising*] What is it?
ALAN: Nothing!

She moves towards him. He turns and moves past her. He is clearly distressed. She contemplates him for a moment.

JILL: [*gently*] Take your sweater off.
ALAN: What?
JILL: I will, if you will.

He stares at her. A pause.
She lifts her sweater over head: he watches—then unzips his. They each remove their shoes, their socks, and their jeans. Then they look at each other diagonally across the square, in which the light is gently increasing.

ALAN: You're . . . You're very . . .
JILL: So are you. . . . [*pause*] Come here.

He goes to her. She comes to him. They meet in the middle, and hold each other, and embrace.

ALAN: [*to Dysart*] She put her mouth in mine. It was lovely!
　　Oh, it was lovely!

They burst into giggles. He lays her gently on the floor in the centre of the square, and bends over her eagerly. Suddenly the noise of Equus fills the place. Hooves smash on wood. Alan straightens up, rigid. He stares straight ahead of him over the prone body of the girl.

DYSART: Yes, what happened then, Alan?

116

ALAN: [to Dysart: brutally] I put it in her!

DYSART: Yes?

ALAN: [to Dysart] I put it in her.

DYSART: You did?

ALAN: [to Dysart] Yes!

DYSART: Was it easy?

ALAN: [to Dysart] Yes.

DYSART: Describe it.

ALAN: [to Dysart] I told you.

DYSART: More exactly.

ALAN: [to Dysart] I put it in her!

DYSART: Did you?

ALAN: [to Dysart] All the way!

DYSART: Did you, Alan?

ALAN: [to Dysart] All the way. I shoved it. I put it in her all the way.

DYSART: Did you?

ALAN: [to Dysart] Yes!

DYSART: Did you?

ALAN: [to Dysart] Yes! . . . Yes!

DYSART: Give me the TRUTH! . . . Did you? . . . *Honestly?*

ALAN: [to Dysart] Fuck off!

He collapses, lying upstage on his face. Jill lies on her back motionless, her head downstage, her arms extended behind her. A pause.

DYSART: [gently] What was it? You couldn't? Though you wanted to very much?

ALAN: [to Dysart] I couldn't . . . see her.

DYSART: What do you mean?

ALAN: [to Dysart] Only Him. Every time I kissed her—*He* was in the way.

DYSART: Who?

Alan turns on his back.

ALAN: [to Dysart] You *know* who! . . . When I touched her, I felt *Him.* Under me . . . His side, waiting for my hand . . . His flanks . . . I refused him. I looked. I looked right at her . . . and I couldn't do it. When

117

I shut my eyes, I saw him at once. The streaks on his belly . . . [*with more desperation*] I couldn't feel *her* flesh at all! I wanted the foam off his neck. His sweaty hide. Not flesh. *Hide! Horse-hide!* . . . Then I couldn't even kiss her.

Jill sits up.

JILL: What is it?
ALAN: [*dodging her hand*] No!

He scrambles up and crouches in the corner against the rails, like a little beast in a cage.

JILL: Alan!
ALAN: Stop it!

Jill gets up.

JILL: It's all right . . . It's all right . . . Don't worry about it. It often happens—honest. . . . There's nothing wrong. I don't mind, you know . . . I don't at all.

He dashes past her downstage.

Alan, look at me . . . Alan? . . . Alan!

He collapses again by the rail.

ALAN: Get out! . . .
JILL: What?
ALAN: [*soft*] Out!
JILL: There's nothing wrong: believe me! It's very common.
ALAN: *Get out!*

He snatches up the invisible pick.

GET OUT!
JILL: Put that down!
ALAN: Leave me alone!

118

JILL: Put that down, Alan. It's very dangerous. Go on, please—drop it.

He 'drops' it, and turns from her.

ALAN: You ever tell anyone. Just you tell . . .
JILL: Who do you think I am? . . . I'm your friend—Alan . . .

She goes towards him.

Listen: you don't have to do anything. Try to realize that. Nothing at all. Why don't we just lie here together in the straw. And talk.
ALAN: [*low*] Please . . .
JILL: Just talk.
ALAN: *Please!*
JILL: All right, I'm going . . . Let me put my clothes on first.

She dresses, hastily.

ALAN: You tell anyone! . . . Just tell and see. . . .
JILL: *Oh, stop it!* . . . I wish you could believe me. It's not in the least important.

Pause.

Anyway, I won't say anything. You know that. You know I won't. . . .

Pause. He stands with his back to her.

Goodnight, then, Alan. . . . I wish—I really wish—

He turns on her, hissing. His face is distorted—possessed. In horrified alarm she turns—fumbles the door open—leaves the barn—shuts the door hard behind her, and dashes up the tunnel out of sight, past the barely visible figure of Nugget.

119

34

Alan stands alone, and naked.
A faint humming and drumming. The boy looks about him
in growing terror.

DYSART: What?
ALAN: [*to Dysart*] He was there. Through the door. The
   door was shut, but he was there! . . . He'd seen every-
   thing. I could hear him. He was laughing.
DYSART: Laughing?
ALAN: [*to Dysart*] Mocking! . . . *Mocking!* . . .

Standing downstage he stares up towards the tunnel. A
great silence weighs on the square.

   [*To the silence: terrified*] Friend . . . Equus the Kind . . .
   The Merciful! . . . *Forgive me!* . . .

Silence.

   It wasn't me. Not really me. Me! . . . Forgive me! . . .
   Take me back again! Please! . . . PLEASE!

He kneels on the downstage lip of the square, still facing
the door, huddling in fear.

   I'll never do it again. I swear . . . I swear! . . .

Silence.

   [*in a moan*] *Please ! ! !* . . .
DYSART: And He? What does He say?
ALAN: [*to Dysart: whispering*] 'Mine! . . . You're mine! . . .
   I am yours and you are mine!' . . . Then I see his eyes.
   They are rolling!

*Nugget begins to advance slowly, with relentless hooves,
down the central tunnel.*

  'I see you. I see you. Always! Everywhere! Forever!'
DYSART: Kiss anyone and I will see?
ALAN: [*to Dysart*] Yes!
DYSART: Lie with anyone and I will see?
ALAN: [*to Dysart*] Yes!
DYSART: And you will fail! Forever and ever you will *fail!*
    You will see ME—and you will FAIL!

*The boy turns round, hugging himself in pain. From the
sides two more horses converge with Nugget on the rails.
Their hooves stamp angrily. The Equus noise is heard
more terribly.*

The Lord thy God is a Jealous God. He sees you. He sees
    you forever and ever, Alan. He sees you! . . . *He sees
    you!*
ALAN: [*in terror*] Eyes! . . . White eyes—never closed!
    Eyes like flames—coming—coming! . . . God seest!
    God seest! . . . NO! . . .

Pause. He steadies himself. The stage begins to blacken.

  [*quieter*] No more. No more, Equus.

*He gets up. He goes to the bench. He takes up the invisible
pick. He moves slowly upstage towards Nugget, concealing
the weapon behind his naked back, in the growing darkness. He stretches out his hand and fondles Nugget's
mask.*

  [*gently*] Equus . . . Noble Equus . . . Faithful and True
  . . . Godslave . . . Thou—God—Seest—NOTHING!

*He stabs out Nugget's eyes. The horse stamps in agony. A
great screaming begins to fill the theatre, growing ever
louder. Alan dashes at the other two horses and blinds them
too, stabbing over the rails. Their metal hooves join in the
stamping.*

Relentlessly, as this happens, three more horses appear in cones of light: not naturalistic animals like the first three, but dreadful creatures out of nightmare. Their eyes flare— their nostrils flare—their mouths flare. They are archetypal images—judging, punishing, pitiless. They do not halt at the rail, but invade the square. As they trample at him, the boy leaps desperately at them, jumping high and naked in the dark, slashing at their heads with arms upraised.
The screams increase. The other horses follow into the square. The whole place is filled with cannoning, blinded horses—and the boy dodging among them, avoiding their slashing hooves at best he can. Finally they plunge off into darkness and away out of sight. The noise dies abruptly, and all we hear is Alan yelling in hysteria as he collapses on the ground—stabbing at his own eyes with the invisible pick.

ALAN: Find me! . . . Find me! . . . Find me! . . .
    KILL ME! . . . KILL ME! . . .

35

The light changes quickly back to brightness.
Dysart enters swiftly, hurls a blanket on the left bench, and rushes over to Alan. The boy is having convulsions on the floor. Dysart grabs his hands, forces them from his eyes, scoops him up in his arms and carries him over to the bench. Alan hurls his arms round Dysart and clings to him, gasping and kicking his legs in dreadful frenzy.
Dysart lays him down and presses his head back on the bench. He keeps talking—urgently talking—soothing the agony as he can.

DYSART: Here . . . Here . . . Ssssh . . . Ssssh . . . Calm now
    . . . Lie back. *Just lie back!* Now breathe in deep. Very
    deep. In . . . Out . . . In . . . Out . . . That's it . . . .
    In. *Out . . In . . . Out . . .*

The boy's breath is drawn into his body with a harsh rasping sound, which slowly grows less. Dysart puts the blanket over him.

Keep it going . . . That's a good boy . . . Very good boy . . . It's all over now, Alan. It's all over. He'll go away now. You'll never see him again, I promise. You'll have no more bad dreams. No more awful nights. Think of that! . . . You are going to be well. I'm going to make you well, I promise you. . . . You'll be here for a while. but I'll be here too, so it won't be so bad. Just trust me . . .

He stands upright. The boy lies still.

Sleep now. Have a good long sleep. You've earned it . . . Sleep. Just sleep. . . . I'm going to make you well.

He steps backwards into the centre of the square. The light brightens some more.
A pause.

DYSART: I'm lying to you, Alan. He won't really go that easily. Just clop away from you like a nice old nag. Oh, no! When Equus leaves—if he leaves at all—it will be with your intestines in his teeth. And I don't stock replacements . . . If you knew anything, you'd get up this minute and run from me fast as you could.

Hesther speaks from her place.

HESTHER: The boy's in pain, Martin.
DYSART: Yes.
HESTHER: And you can take it away.
DYSART: Yes.
HESTHER: Then that has to be enough for you, surely? . . . In the end!
DYSART: [*crying out*] All right! I'll take it away! He'll be delivered from madness. *What then?* He'll feel himself acceptable! *What then?* Do you think feelings like his can be simply re-attached, like plasters? Stuck on to other objects we select? *Look at him!* . . . My desire

123

might be to make this boy an ardent husband—a caring citizen—a worshipper of abstract and unifying God. My achievement, however, is more likely to make a ghost! . . . Let me tell you exactly what I'm going to do to him!

He steps out of the square and walks round the upstage end of it, storming at the audience.

I'll heal the rash on his body. I'll erase the welts cut into his mind by flying manes. When that's done, I'll set him on a nice mini-scooter and send him puttering off into the Normal world where animals are treated *properly:* made extinct, or put into servitude, or tethered all their lives in dim light, just to feed it! I'll give him the good Normal world where we're tethered beside them— blinking our nights away in a nonstop drench of cathode-ray over our shrivelling heads! I'll take away his Field of Ha Ha, and give him Normal places for his ecstasy— multi-lane highways driven through the guts of cities, extinguishing Place altogether, *even the idea of Place!* He'll trot on his metal pony tamely through the concrete evening—and one thing I promise you: he will never touch hide again! With any luck his private parts will come to feel as plastic to him as the products of the factory to which he will almost certainly be sent. Who knows? He may even come to find sex funny. Smirky funny. Bit of grunt funny. Trampled and furtive and entirely in control. Hopefully, he'll feel nothing at his fork but Approved Flesh. *I doubt, however, with much passion!* . . . Passion, you see, can be destroyed by a doctor. It cannot be created.

He addresses Alan directly, in farewell.

You won't gallop any more, Alan. Horses will be quite safe. You'll save your pennies every week, till you can change that scooter in for a car, and put the odd fifty P on the gee-gees, quite forgetting that they were ever anything more to you than bearers of little

124

profits and little losses. You will, however, be without pain. More or less completely without pain.

Pause.
He speaks directly to the theatre, standing by the motion-less body of Alan Strang, under the blanket.

And now for me it never stops: that voice of Equus out of the cave—'Why Me? . . . Why Me? . . . Account for Me!' . . . All right—I surrender! I say it . . . In an ultimate sense I cannot know what I do in this place—yet I do ultimate things. Essentially I cannot know what I do—yet I do essential things. Irreversible, terminal things. I stand in the dark with a pick in my hand, striking at heads!

He moves away from Alan, back to the downstage bench, and finally sits.

I need—more desperately than my children need me—a way of seeing in the dark. What way is this? . . . *What dark is this?* . . . I cannot call it ordained of God: I can't get that far. I will however pay it so much homage. There is now, in my mouth, this sharp chain. And it never comes out.

A long pause.
Dysart sits staring.

BLACKOUT

BARD BOOKS

DISTINGUISHED DRAMA

ARMS AND THE MAN George Bernard Shaw	01628	.60
CANDIDE Lillian Hellman	12211	1.65
THE CHANGING ROOM, HOME, THE CONTRACTOR: THREE PLAYS David Storey	22772	2.45
DANTON'S DEATH Georg Büchner	10876	1.25
A DREAM PLAY August Strindberg	18655	.75
EDWARD II Christopher Marlowe	18648	.75
THE FANTASTICKS Tom Jones and Harvey Schmidt	22129	1.65
GHOSTS Henrik Ibsen	22152	.95
HEDDA GABLER Henrik Ibsen	24620	.95
THE IMPORTANCE OF BEING EARNEST Oscar Wilde	21162	.95
THE LOWER DEPTHS Maxim Gorky	18630	.75
MISS JULIE August Strindberg	19018	.70
THE PLAYBOY OF THE WESTERN WORLD John Millington Synge	22046	.95
THE SEA GULL Anton Chekhov	24638	.95
THE THREE SISTERS Anton Chekhov	19844	.75
UNCLE VANYA Anton Chekhov	18663	.75
THE WILD DUCK Henrik Ibsen	23093	.95
WOYZECK Georg Büchner	10751	1.25

 **BARD BOOKS**

the classics, poetry, drama and distinguished modern fiction

A SELECTION OF RECENT TITLES

FICTION

BILLIARDS AT HALF-PAST NINE Heinrich Böll	23390	1.75
THE CABALA Thornton Wilder	24653	1.75
THE CLOWN Heinrich Böll	24471	1.75
DANGLING MAN Saul Bellow	24463	1.65
THE EYE OF THE HEART Barbara Howes, Ed.	20883	2.25
HEAVEN'S MY DESTINATION Thornton Wilder	23416	1.65
HERMAPHRODEITY Alan Friedman	16865	2.45
THE MAZE MAKER Michael Ayrton	23648	1.65
THE RECOGNITIONS William Gaddis	18572	2.65
THE VICTIM Saul Bellow	24273	1.95
THE WOMAN OF ANDROS Thornton Wilder	23416	1.65

DRAMA

THE CHANGING ROOM, HOME, **THE CONTRACTOR: THREE PLAYS** David Storey	22772	2.45

POETRY

YEVTUSHENKO'S READER Yevgeny Yevtushenko	14811	1.45

Where better paperbacks are sold, or directly from the publisher. Include 25¢ per copy for mailing; allow three weeks for delivery.

Avon Books, Mail Order Dept.
250 West 55th Street, New York, N. Y. 10019

BC 7-75

BARD BOOKS

distinguished poetry

EVANGELINE
Henry Wadsworth Longfellow   01669   .60

LEAVES OF GRASS   Walt Whitman   02154   .60

THE RIME OF THE ANCIENT MARINER
Samuel Taylor Coleridge   24331   .95

THE RUBAIYAT OF OMAR KHAYYAM
Edward Fitzgerald   18770   .70

SHAKESPEARE'S SONNETS
Ed. by Barbara Herrnstein Smith   08904   1.25

A SHROPSHIRE LAD   A. E. Housman   02139   .60

**SONGS OF INNOCENCE AND OF
EXPERIENCE**   William Blake   18762   .70

SONNETS FROM THE PORTUGUESE
Elizabeth B. Browning   19836   .75

YEVTUSHENKO'S READER
Yevgeny Yevtushenko   14811   1.45
